small railroads YOU can build

EDITED BY BOB HAYDEN

Building the Bantam & Cycloid Railroad page 25

APARTMENT dwellers take note: This layout was built on the kitchen table —in the kitchen! No space is *too* small if you're determined.

From Train Set to Model Railroad page 32

IDEAL for a family project, the Marquette & Independence Railroad starts with a train set and progresses to a busy short line that features a compact yard, locomotive facilities, and switching action.

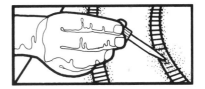

Space-Saving Layout Storage Ideas page 46

INGENUITY is the answer when you're faced with no room for a model railroad. Here are thought-provoking designs for layouts that lift, fold, flip, and rotate out of the way.

The Rubble Creek & Thunder Mine Railroad page 48

TRY this for size—an N gauge layout built to fit in a closet, with the clothes!

MODEL RAILROAD HANDBOOK NO. 9

Some of the material in this book has been edited and updated from articles that first appeared in MODEL RAILROADER magazine.

ART DIRECTOR: Lawrence Luser
LAYOUT: William Scholz
CONTINUITY: Mike Schafer
PHOTOGRAPHY: Jim Hediger, Walt Olsen, A.L. Schmidt

KALMBACH **K**BOOKS.

First printing, 1978. Second printing, 1979. Third printing, 1981. Fourth printing, 1983. Fifth printing, 1986. Sixth printing, 1988. Seventh printing, 1989. Eighth printing, 1991.

Get Started With a Small Layout

The beginning of the world's best— and most diversified—hobby for you

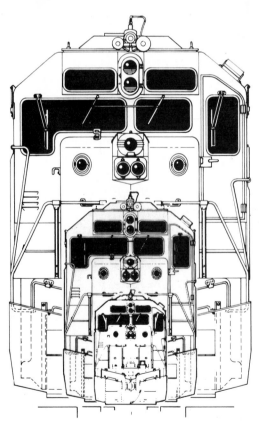

The three most popular sizes of railroad models: (top to bottom) O, HO, and N.

MODEL RAILROADING is a dynamic, year-round leisure-time activity. Sure, your model railroading enthusiasm may reach a high point during the winter months and the traditional holiday season—when Christmastime gift-giving often includes train sets and accessory items—but you can enjoy the hobby just as much when blistering summer heat forces you inside to a cool basement or air-conditioned family room.

This book is an introduction to the wide world of scale model railroading beyond the simple train set oval of track, and an introduction that involves YOU. Its premise is that the best way to get started in this hobby is to build a *small* model railroad, a layout of modest dimensions that you can build step-by-step, following proven techniques and using proven materials. Even if you have the space, time, and budget to build a much larger layout, get off on the right foot by building a little pike first, to sample the many facets of layout building and to develop the skills you'll need for a more extensive project. If you're a veteran model railroader between permanent homes or permanent layouts, a small portable railroad may be just what you need to keep your interest kindled and give you a chance to try new techniques and materials.

The stories brought together here were selected for their clear explanations of construction methods. Each project layout is divided into easy steps, and no phase of construction —carpentry, trackwork, wiring, or scenery —is so time-consuming that it becomes tedious. Each of the three major projects is intended to have you running trains on the railroad in less than a week of evening work. Two of the project layouts are HO scale, the most popular model railroading size, and the other is N scale, second in popularity. Also included are advice on how to set up and operate train sets, construction details for building two sturdy train tables, and information on ways to store a small railroad where space is at an absolute premium.

Materials

You'll find shopping lists—Bills of Materials—throughout the book. The lists are arranged to support each phase of construction, so you can spread out your purchases to suit your budget and yet keep up the momentum of the work. You'll find your Number One source of supplies and information is your hobby shop. Other items come from hardware stores, lumber yards, and consumer electrical and electronics supply stores like Radio Shack, Allied, Lafayette, and

Olson Electronics. If you live in an area where this kind of store, and perhaps the hobby shop, is a long way away, check MODEL RAILROADER magazine for mail-order supply houses.

Where to work—and how

You can build your small railroad anywhere. In fact, the Bantam & Cycloid project that starts on page 25 was built on a kitchen table, *in the kitchen.* Wherever you work, cover surfaces that can be damaged by paint, plaster, glue, or tools with newspaper, old sheets, or disposable plastic drop cloths.

Because the tasks involved are simple, safe, and enjoyable, building a small railroad is an excellent activity for family participation. The best construction advice is TAKE YOUR TIME—this hobby is for fun and relaxation, and hurrying through the work enhances neither. For more advice, check first with the people at the hobby shop. It's likely that they are model railroaders themselves and it's their business to hear your problems and help with them. If they are stumped, chances are you'll look for the answer with them in one of Kalmbach's extensive line of model railroad how-to answer books. A list of these books is on the inside back cover.

Finally, when you've built a small railroad like the ones in this book, be proud of it and show it off to others. Model railroaders are not hypercritical people—they're active hobbyists and they've made most of the mistakes. They'll be eager to see your pike and to hear your ideas. Showing off your layout means photographs, too, and if you can take clear, sharp pictures of your railroad, send them along to MODEL RAILROADER magazine so that other modelers nationwide can see and appreciate your work.

Tools

A basic model railroad tool box

You'll need only a few common hand tools to build the project small railroads shown in the pages that follow, and if you're a homeowner, chances are you already have most of the required implements.

Woodworking tools:
 Claw hammer
 1/4" hand (or power*) drill
 Twist drill set, fractional, 1/16"—1/4"
 Countersink bit for flathead wood screws
 Hand crosscut saw (or power Saber saw*)
 6" screwdriver
 Measuring tape or yardstick

Trackwork and wiring tools
 1/16" nail set
 Thin needle files
 Modeler's knife
 Needle-nose pliers
 3" screwdriver (for wire terminals)
 Razor saw**
 Flush-cutting nippers**
 Motor tool with abrasive cutoff disks**
 Pin vise with No. 61 through No. 80 drills**
 Soldering iron or gun and resin-core solder**
 Wire strippers**
 *Optional
 **Needed only for flexible track and some wiring schemes. Rail cutting and soldering are not required for most layouts.

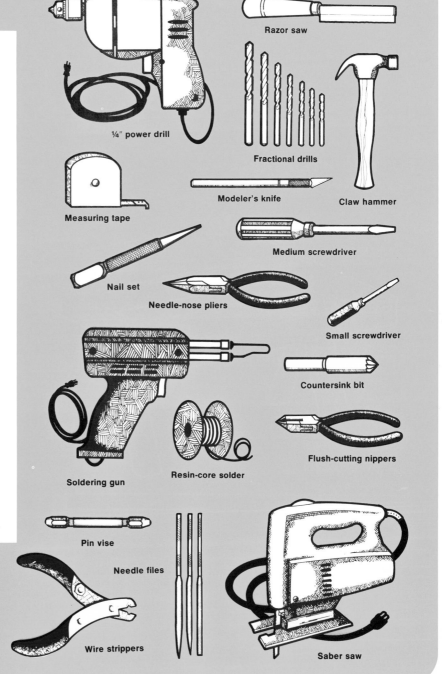

1/4" power drill

Measuring tape

Nail set

Needle-nose pliers

Soldering gun

Resin-core solder

Razor saw

Fractional drills

Modeler's knife

Claw hammer

Medium screwdriver

Small screwdriver

Countersink bit

Flush-cutting nippers

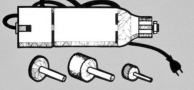

Motor tool

Pin vise

Needle files

Wire strippers

Saber saw

Two Easy-to-Build 4 x 8 Layout Tables

Try butt-jointed construction, or use L-Girder techniques

BOTH designs shown on these pages will get your layout up off the floor and on its way to becoming an operating model railroad. The 4 x 8 plywood sheet is the standard size sold by lumber dealers. The solid tabletop is ideal for a first layout because it can be assembled with only a few tools—saw, drill, hammer, measuring tape or yardstick, and screwdriver—and requires little carpentry before starting trackwork, wiring, and scenery.

Table height

Before you purchase materials, consider how high you want the table. A height of 40-48 inches—several inches higher than the average table or desk—is preferred for an adult. Higher layouts look more realistic, but those above 50" become difficult to work on without standing on some kind of platform.

Lumber

Common-grade pine is adequate for framework. Utility-grade plywood, plugged and sanded on one side, is fine for the table top because it will be covered by scenery. Try to choose lumber that is reasonably straight and free from large knots along the edges. If you do not have a saw, some lumber dealers will cut pieces to length for you for a small fee.

Advantages and disadvantages

Butt-jointed framework is best for a layout that must be portable. The frame and top can remain separate from the legs, and the layout can be stored leaning against a wall where it takes up very little space. The only disadvantage of the butt-jointed system is that the cross members (B) must be accurately cut to the same length.

The L-girder design brings the advantage of greater strength, but is thicker and heavier than the butt-jointed framework. L-girder framework is very sturdy with or without the plywood top, and it is the framework design most often chosen for extensive layouts.

BUTT-JOINTED TABLE CONSTRUCTION DETAILS

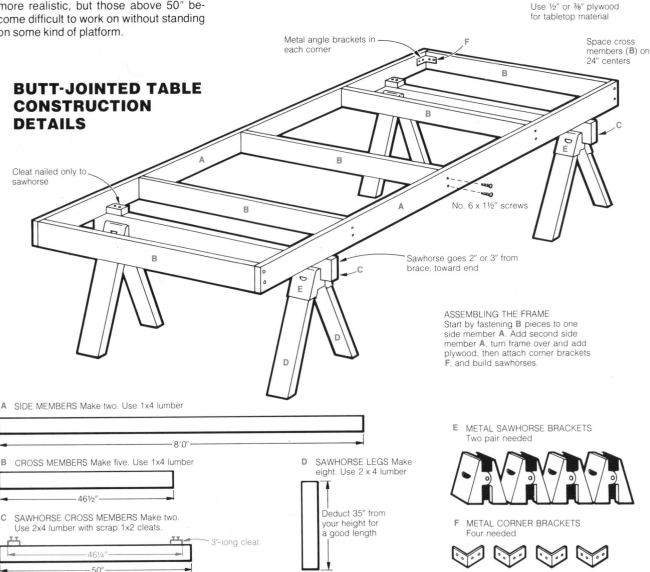

Use ½" or ⅜" plywood for tabletop material

Metal angle brackets in each corner

Space cross members (B) on 24" centers

Cleat nailed only to sawhorse

No. 6 x 1½" screws

Sawhorse goes 2" or 3" from brace, toward end

ASSEMBLING THE FRAME
Start by fastening **B** pieces to one side member **A**. Add second side member **A**, turn frame over and add plywood, then attach corner brackets **F**, and build sawhorses.

A SIDE MEMBERS Make two. Use 1x4 lumber
— 8'0" —

B CROSS MEMBERS Make five. Use 1x4 lumber
— 46½" —

C SAWHORSE CROSS MEMBERS Make two. Use 2x4 lumber with scrap 1x2 cleats.
3"-long cleat
— 46¼" —
— 50" —

D SAWHORSE LEGS Make eight. Use 2 x 4 lumber
Deduct 35" from your height for a good length

E METAL SAWHORSE BRACKETS Two pair needed

F METAL CORNER BRACKETS Four needed

L-GIRDER TABLE CONSTRUCTION DETAILS

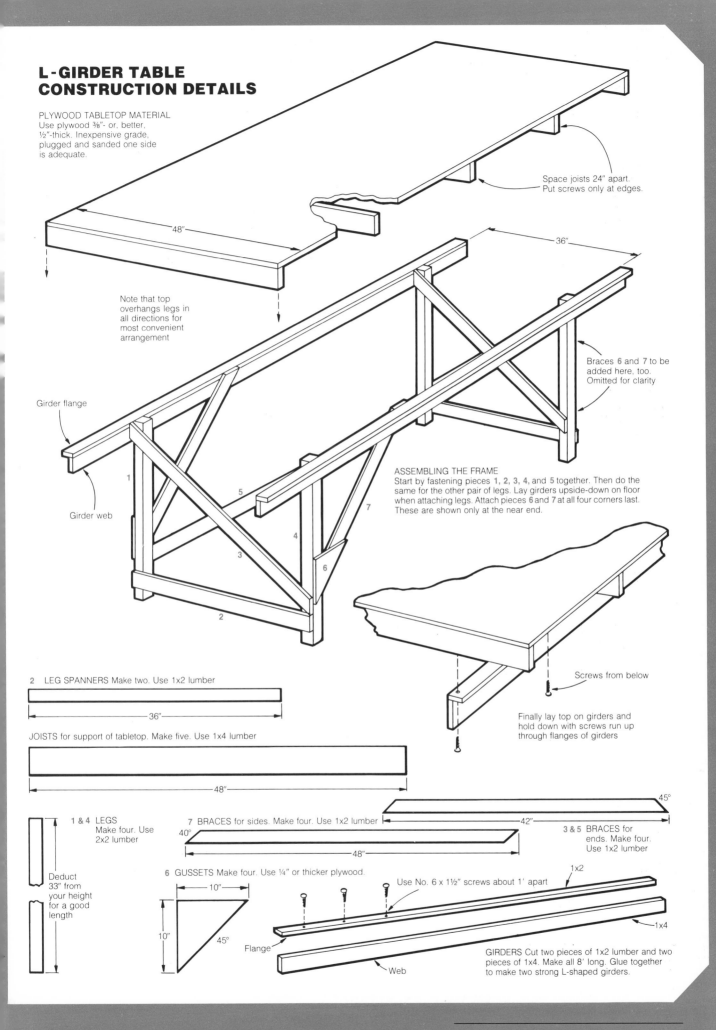

PLYWOOD TABLETOP MATERIAL Use plywood ⅜"- or, better, ½"-thick. Inexpensive grade, plugged and sanded one side is adequate.

Space joists 24" apart. Put screws only at edges.

48"

36"

Note that top overhangs legs in all directions for most convenient arrangement

Girder flange

Girder web

Braces **6** and **7** to be added here, too. Omitted for clarity

ASSEMBLING THE FRAME Start by fastening pieces **1**, **2**, **3**, **4**, and **5** together. Then do the same for the other pair of legs. Lay girders upside-down on floor when attaching legs. Attach pieces **6** and **7** at all four corners last. These are shown only at the near end.

Screws from below

Finally lay top on girders and hold down with screws run up through flanges of girders

2 LEG SPANNERS Make two. Use 1x2 lumber

36"

JOISTS for support of tabletop. Make five. Use 1x4 lumber

48"

1 & 4 LEGS Make four. Use 2x2 lumber

Deduct 33" from your height for a good length

7 BRACES for sides. Make four. Use 1x2 lumber

40°

48"

45°

42"

3 & 5 BRACES for ends. Make four. Use 1x2 lumber

6 GUSSETS Make four. Use ¼" or thicker plywood.

10"

10"

45°

Flange

Use No. 6 x 1½" screws about 1' apart

1x2

1x4

Web

GIRDERS Cut two pieces of 1x2 lumber and two pieces of 1x4. Make all 8' long. Glue together to make two strong L-shaped girders.

What to do when you have to buy more track

Installing the train set around the Christmas tree

How a typewriter eraser makes trains run better

All's not lost if a car falls and breaks

Train Set Questions and Answers

BY BOB HAYDEN

TRAIN SETS come in all popular scales. They are sold both as toys and starter outfits for scale model railroading. Some sets have very good instructions, others come with only very basic information. To start you off on the right foot with your set—or to help you solve problems that have already arisen—here are answers to the most-asked questions from beginners.

Setting up your train set

• **How should I go about setting up the train set track and the other equipment?**

First, if your set has an instruction sheet, READ THE INSTRUCTIONS. This can save you from ruining something, or from taking things apart several times to get the assembly right. If the parts of your set came packaged in several small boxes inside a larger box, check each for instructions and take inventory. Begin assembling the pieces,

step-by-step, and TAKE YOUR TIME. Don't throw the boxes away; if you aren't going to build a permanent railroad right away they offer storage protection for your equipment.

• **What tools will I need?**

Some sets are engineered to go together without any tools, but usually you'll need a screwdriver with a $3/16$"- or $1/4$"-wide blade to attach wires to the track and power-pack terminals. The second tool you should have is a pair of inexpensive needle-nose pliers.

• **Is there anything I should do to the equipment before I run it? Do I have to oil the engine?**

The locomotive and cars should be ready to go right from the box. When you unpack the equipment, check carefully for bits of paper, inspection tags, or packing materials that could interfere with moving parts. Don't lubricate *anything*. There should be sufficient grease and oil on the moving parts for

many hours of operation. Excess lubricants get onto the wheels and track where they mix with dust to form a black caked deposit that interferes with electrical contact and good operation.

Track

• **Can I run my train set on the floor?**

Yes, but you shouldn't leave it there for long. Bits of dust and fibers get into the moving parts of the equipment, and this will eventually bring everything to a halt. You'll need, at a minimum, a small sheet of hardboard or plywood for track support, even if you don't nail your track sections to it. Some kind of off-the-floor support—a small table, sawhorses, even two chairs—is a big step toward trouble-free operation.

• **What should I look for when I put the track sections together?**

Be careful with the rail joiners, those little channels of formed metal that hold the track pieces together. Make sure the mating rail end goes inside, not on top of, the rail joiner. If the joiner is free to slide back and forth on the joint, make sure half of it is on each section. If you distort one of the joiners, replace it; spares are sold at hobby shops. Above all, don't force the track parts together. If the sections don't slip together something is wrong, so examine the pieces under a bright light and correct the problem before going on.

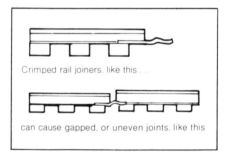

Crimped rail joiners, like this . . .

can cause gapped, or uneven joints, like this

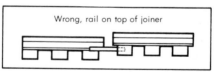

Wrong, rail on top of joiner

• **My train runs OK, but it always goes off the track at one point. What causes this?**

Derailments are usually caused by misalignment at a track joint. Check first to see that all track sections are firmly pushed together, with no wide gaps at the joints. Run your finger across the joints to look for roughness or height mismatches, and read the box on "Rail joints and switch points" on page 38 for the remedy. Occasionally, the manufacturing machines that make the track sections impart a banana bend to the pieces (see figure). You can remove this distortion by very gently bending both ends of the track down while supporting the middle on the edge of a table or counter top.

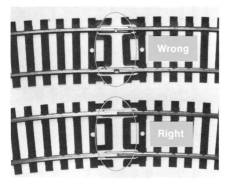

Left: To prevent damage to rail joiners when assembling your track, hold the sections against a smooth surface and gently slip them together. Right: Loose and misaligned rail joints are the greatest cause of derailments. The track sections at the top have gaps between the rail ends and there is a definite kink in the curve. The lower sections are properly mated.

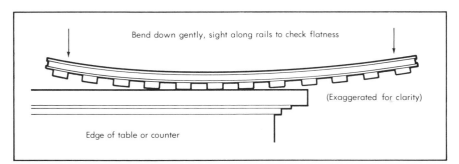

Bend down gently, sight along rails to check flatness

(Exaggerated for clarity)

Edge of table or counter

• **Do I have to stay with the brand of track furnished with my train set, or are several brands compatible?**

In HO, most brands will mate properly with one another, but in other scales it is a different story. Even in HO

some brands have thicker ties than others, making for minor differences in height at rail joints. When you buy more track, take a section of your train set track with you to the store, and check that it fits with what you buy.

Power pack and wiring

• **Can the electricity in the track harm the kids or the family pet?**

No. The power pack output is low voltage and low current, so it's safe. But because it does plug into the wall outlet, your power pack deserves the same respect you give any small electrical appliance. Unplug the pack while you are connecting or disconnecting wires at the terminals, and leave it unplugged when you are not operating the trains.

• **My set came without a power pack. What kind should I buy? Can I use an old toy train transformer?**

The train set instructions should tell you what kind of power pack to buy. Take the locomotive to your hobby shop and show it to the people there. Scale model train sets usually require direct current (d.c.), so your toy train transformer won't work unless it has a variable d.c. output. The alternating current (a.c.) output of most toy train transformers will ruin the motor in an HO or N scale locomotive.

When you purchase a power pack, don't purchase the least expensive model. One of the better-quality packs will last a lifetime and you can consider it an investment. A pack with a rotating speed control will hold up better than one with a sliding control, and a circuit breaker is a must to protect your equipment and the pack from damage.

• **There are two sets of terminals on the back of my power pack. You said I** should hook up the track to the d.c. terminals, so what are the others for?

Most power packs provide 16-18 volts a.c. to run accessories such as remote switch machines, structure lights, and animated crossing gates.

These power pack terminals are clearly marked, but if your pack lacks a "track" label, just make sure you connect the wires from the track to the *variable d.c.* terminals.

• **How much track can my train set power pack handle? How large a layout can I build before I need to buy a larger pack?**

The size of your power pack, electrically speaking, is its capacity in amperes (amps). Most of the small packs included or sold for use with train sets have a capacity of one amp or less, enough to run one engine. When the engine is heavily loaded (a long train), or when two or more engines are run on the same train, the capacity of the pack may be exceeded, tripping the circuit breaker. Except on very large layouts, the amount of track is not what is limited by the size of the power pack, but rather the number of engines that can run at one time, or the number of cars that one powerful engine can pull. You'll need a *larger* power pack to run several engines on the same train and you'll need *additional* power packs to run trains independent of one another.

• **My loop of track worked well for a couple of weeks, but then one track section seemed to go dead. My engine runs okay on the rest of the layout, but won't budge on the bad section.**

Check the rail joiners at each end of the dead section. First be sure that the rail joiners are touching the rails on both sides of the joints. If the joiners are loose or spread from repeated assembly, squeeze them gently with needle-nose pliers until they make good contact with the sides of the rails. If the rail ends are tarnished where they contact the joiners, polish them with a scrap of sandpaper, a typewriter eraser, or the fine side of an emery board.

Your Locomotive

• **When I put my locomotive on the track it won't run unless I push it, and then it stalls halfway around the track.**

This sounds like dirty track and dirty pickup wheels on the locomotive. Hobby

shops usually carry several types of track cleaners. One of the best is an eraserlike, abrasive-impregnated rubber block that you rub on the tops of the rails to remove dirt and oxide. Clean the locomotive wheels with a cotton swab moistened with rubbing alcohol, being careful not to get any fluid on the painted body shell.

• **My engine doesn't run at all.**

If you have some experience at assembling and repairing things that have lots of small parts, unscrew or unsnap the locomotive body shell and look for something obvious like a disconnected wire. If you find nothing, take the locomotive to your local hobby shop for repair. If the problem is minor, the repairman might be able to fix it on the spot and show you what caused the trouble.

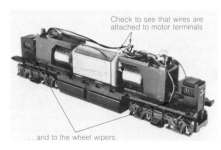

Check to see that wires are attached to motor terminals

... and to the wheel wipers.

If your loco doesn't run, check it to ensure that all wires are firmly connected and that all snap-together assemblies are properly and fully mated. This diesel mechanism is HO gauge.

Rolling stock

• **One of the cars in my train dropped onto the floor and broke a coupler and one of the wheels. Can I get new parts or do I have to buy a whole new car?**

Most damage like you describe is pretty easy to fix. Take the car to your hobby store and buy the parts, and you'll have the fun of fixing the car yourself.

• **If I buy additional cars for my set, will they couple with the ones I already have?**

Yes. There are exceptions, but in HO, almost all ready-to-run and kit equipment comes with horn-hook couplers, while the standard in N is the Rapido coupler. Here again, the best advice is to take along one of the cars you have to compare with the new ones.

Couplers

• **One of the cars in my set won't couple when I back the other cars up to it, and it often uncouples from the train when I don't want it to. Why?**

One of the couplers is sticking. Try to free it by moving it from side to side or up and down. All of your couplers will work better if you puff just a little fine powdered graphite from a tube dispenser into the coupler pocket.

• **The part of the coupler that hangs down below the hook catches in the track at switches and rerailer sections**

and derails the train. How can I fix this?

The coupler actuating pins on hook-type couplers can be clipped off without affecting the automatic coupling action. If you want automatic *un*coupling, the best thing to do is convert your equipment to Kadee brand magnetic couplers (available in N, HO, and O scales).

• **Is buying a train set the only way to get started in scale model railroading?**

Far from it. Some HO "pick and choose" trains made up from several manufacturers' products are shown in the box on page 17, and you can do the same in N scale. Train sets are an easy way to purchase most of what you need in one place, and they offer a small savings over purchasing the individual components.

• **Are there any special things I should do to set up the train around the Christmas tree?**

First put down a good flat surface for the track —a sheet of plywood at least 3 inches bigger all around than the track loop is ideal. If you have a live tree with a stand that holds water, put the power pack in a location where the water can't spill on it if the stand is tilted or tipped. Make sure the power pack isn't closed in or covered; it must have adequate ventilation for cooling. If you can, nail the track sections to the baseboard with ½-inch No. 19 wire brads, but if you don't nail the pieces down, at least join them together with masking tape placed on the bottom of the ties. Vacuum the track when you clean the rest of the room.

Clean your track with an abrasive track cleaner block or a typewriter eraser, and if you aren't setting up a permanent layout, add strips of masking tape to the bottom of the ties as shown.

Couplers won't work if they stick, so exercise them with your finger to free them, and add a little powdered graphite from a "puff tube" dispenser to keep them reliable.

Start running HO trains in less than a week

How a central ridge makes 4x6 seem much larger

Four spurs and two trains—without a control panel

Featherweight mountains formed with a rasp

Why even the rails get painted

A town left in the desert and a mineful of fun

Building the Yule Central Railway

BY BOB HAYDEN

THE Yule Central is a 4 x 6-foot HO layout that you can build in just a few weeks of evenings, but that incorporates the features of layouts many times its size. Although the layout is easy to build with today's snap-together sectional track and plug-in wiring components, there's still enough challenge to help you develop your craftsmanship and lead to a true feeling of accomplishment.

You can build this railroad as a Christmastime display and then add scenery and structures to turn the pike into a realistic scale model railroad, or you can build it as an individual or family hobby project at some other time of the year—perhaps during the summer season, out-of-doors. Even if you have no experience in modelbuilding or model railroading, our step-by-step approach will have you out of your armchair and running trains in less than a week, and in a month of evenings you can become the proud superintendent of a layout replete with structures, scenery, and maybe even an addition!

Any HO train set can serve as the foundation for building the Yule Central, or you can purchase the components individually, picking and choosing your locomotive and cars from the vast range of ready-to-run and kit models. To help if you decide to use the latter approach, I've put together six trains that operate well and look appropriate on the layout (see box, page 17).

Materials for building the layout are divided into four lists, one each for layout table parts, track and wiring components, scenery items, and suggested structures. You can purchase the materials all at once, or you can divide expenditures into four installments; each list includes everything needed for the associated major construction step. The material lists also include suggested tools; most of them are common household implements.

The track plan

The Yule Central's 18"-radius curves will allow you to operate the great majority of HO ready-to-run and kit-built rolling stock, everything but extra-long freight and passenger cars and huge locomotives that wouldn't be appropriate on a short line anyway. The center area of the track plan is open, a perfect place for the traditional Christmas tree—and for a small town and rugged scenic ridge after the holiday season. The track plan features a smooth loop for display and round-and-round running, a passing siding where one train can meet and run past another, and three spurs where freight cars can be spotted to pick up or deliver their loads. The interchange track along the front edge of the layout gives the Yule Central a connection with an imaginary larger railroad. This interchange connection justifies the variety of cars that you can operate on the layout, because it "connects" the Yule Central with the outside world. The plan also provides for logical, planned expansion later: The interchange track is positioned so it can connect with a yard or even a larger layout. More about that later.

Let's get started

All talk never built a railroad, lifesize or model, so let's get started. First find a place to set up the layout and a place to do your construction work. You can—and other enterprising modelers have—set up your railroad on a spare table, a pool table, a ping-pong table, or on sawhorses as I did. Remember when choosing your "site" that if you build your layout in a room not purposely set aside for hobby activity you must protect the table and flooring. Building the Yule Central is not a particularly messy job, but you can't avoid the possibility of spilling something simply by promising yourself that you'll be extra careful—invest in a heavy-duty plastic painter's drop cloth to cover the area under the layout, and you'll be able to make the same mistakes I did without causing any damage. It's important to be a good tenant, so keep a supply of newspapers, rags, and paper towels handy in the construction area. The extra time it takes to execute a job neatly can be chalked up to good "community relations" for your new railroad.

Track, benchwork, and sawhorses

The tabletop platform that is the base for the Yule Central is neither preci-

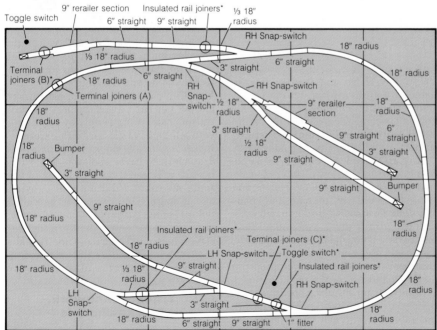

Toggle switch
9" rerailer section
6" straight
9" straight
Insulated rail joiners*
⅓ 18" radius
RH Snap-switch
18" radius
⅓ 18" radius
18" radius
6" straight
18" radius
Terminal joiners (B)*
Terminal joiners (A)
6" straight
3" straight
6" straight
RH Snap-switch
RH Snap-switch
½ 18" radius
9" rerailer section
18" radius
3" straight
9" straight
6" straight
18" radius
½ 18" radius
9" straight
3" straight
9" straight
Bumper
18" radius
Bumper
3" straight
18" radius
9" straight
9" straight
18" radius
18" radius
Insulated rail joiners*
Terminal joiners (C)*
18" radius
LH Snap-switch
Toggle switch*
18" radius
⅓ 18" radius
9" straight
Insulated rail joiners*
18" radius
RH Snap-switch
LH Snap-switch
3" straight
18" radius
18" radius
6" straight
9" straight
1" fitter
18" radius

Fig. 1 TRACK PLAN   * For fancy wiring only   Grid squares are 12"

sion-built nor beautiful to look at, but it gets your railroad up off the floor, and it's what goes on *top* that counts. Cut the lumber to the sizes indicated in the list of materials, and measure two feet in from each end of the six-foot-long side pieces to mark the positions of the intermediate cross members. Drill two $5/64''$ holes in the side pieces on the centerline of each cross member and use the countersink bit to make recesses for the screw heads. Join one side piece to one end cross member first, then add the other end and side to form the rectangular outside frame. Next, add the intermediate cross members. Drive the screws in until the heads are flush with the surface of the sides; a little bar soap rubbed on the screw threads will make them go in easier. Use white glue in all the joints.

Now turn the framework over and position your plywood sheet on top of it, lining up the edges and equalizing any overhang. Drill and countersink $5/64''$ holes at one-foot intervals around the

Above: Your first step in building the Yule Central is assembly of this simple frame from 1 x 2 lumber. Build the frame on a hard, flat floor, then turn it over and attach the plywood tabletop to the "even" side. Frame, top, and sawhorse construction should take less than one evening. Below: This eagle's-eye view shows how little space the layout takes up when leaned against a wall for storage. Because it was designed with portability in mind, the pike can be moved quickly and easily by two people.

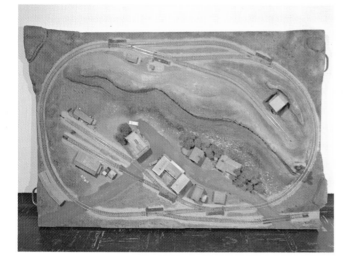

LAYOUT TABLE PARTS

Sawhorses

8	common grade pine, 2 x 4 x 3'-4"* (legs)
2	common grade pine, 2 x 4 x 4'-2"* (cross members)
2 pr.	metal sawhorse brackets
2 doz.	6D x 1½" common nails
4 doz.	8D x 2" common nails

Benchwork

1 sheet	4' x 6' x ⅜" fir plywood, plugged and sanded, good one side
2	common grade pine, 1 x 2 x 6'* (side pieces)
4	common grade pine, 1 x 2 x 3'-10½"* (cross members)
4	2½" metal corner braces
2 doz.	¾" No. 8 flathead wood screws
2 doz.	1½" No. 8 flathead wood screws
3 doz.	1" No. 6 flathead wood screws
4	6¾" heavy-duty door pulls (handles), optional

white glue

medium-grit sandpaper

*Many lumber dealers will cut lumber to length for a small fee. This speeds construction, requires fewer tools, and makes your materials easier to transport.

Tools required: Screwdriver, hammer, ruler/tape measure, 5/64" twist drill bit, countersink bit, hand or power drill, hand or portable power saw (needed only if lumber is not purchased cut to length)

In this overall view of the "front" side of the layout the interchange track is in the right foreground, the town of Yule (pronounced "you-lee") occupies the center area, and the mine tipple just shows behind the high central scenic ridge. If you haven't guessed, the "Yule" in Yule Central is the misspelled name of one of the Chinese workers who built the railroad.

perimeter of the plywood. Fasten the plywood sheet to the framework with 1" No. 6 flathead wood screws. Also, drill holes, countersink, and drive 1" No. 6 screws into the intermediate cross members at one-foot intervals. You'll find the ⅜" plywood lends a great deal of strength to your framework, which makes it possible to use the light, inexpensive 1 x 2 stock.

Add 2½" metal corner braces using ¾" No. 8 flathead screws on the inside of each corner to strengthen the framework, and your layout base is complete. The handles are optional; they help immeasurably when moving the layout, and if you don't add them you'll wish you had.

Assemble the sawhorses from 2 x 4 stock, following the instructions packaged with your sawhorse brackets. The leg length in the material list results in a tabletop height of 44 inches. This is a convenient stand-up working height for an adult, but you may want to shorten the legs to lower the layout if there's a youngster in your crew or if you prefer to work sitting down. Beveling the ends of the legs that touch the floor will make the sawhorses less likely to wobble.

Place the layout platform on top of your sawhorses and admire your handiwork. I found that the layout base has no tendency to move from side to side, but you may want to nail small wood chocks on the ends of the sawhorse cross members to serve as anchors.

To complete your benchwork, wrap medium-grit sandpaper around a scrap of lumber and sand the plywood sheet to remove splinters and to round edges and corners so clothing won't snag on them.

If you haven't done so already, set up a temporary oval of track on your platform, hook up leads from your power pack, and take time out to run the train over your new "landscape."

Locating the track parts

Use fig. 1 as a guide to assemble the track parts on the table top. Don't worry about inserting insulated and terminal rail joiners yet, just assemble the parts according to the plan. Note the location of the 1″ fitter section. If you use a different brand of sectional track than I did, you may have to use a different length from the track assortment to make the overall plan come out even, but try to use as few fitter sections as

possible. If you modify the Yule Central track plan or redesign your own layout, try to stick with standard-length track sections. Fewer sections means fewer rail joints and fewer chances for misalignment and derailment.

Go over the assembled track at least twice to make sure all joints are tightly closed and properly aligned. If you've used the right track sections in the right places you shouldn't have to force anything. Make sure the track is properly positioned relative to the edges of the benchwork, and use a fine-point felt-tip pen to mark the track centerline between each pair of ties. We'll use these centerlines to position the cork roadbed strip, so take your time and make sure the marks are accurate. At the same time, make light pencil notes on the plywood showing where rail joints fall and where each track section goes. Make these notes at least an inch out from the centerline, so they'll still be visible after we install the roadbed. This notation will save confusion later when you lay the track on top of the roadbed.

Take the sections apart, being careful not to distort or twist any of the rail joiners. Put the track aside, and use a rag or whisk broom to sweep the plywood surface. Separate the halves of a cork roadbed strip and begin nailing one half in place against the track centerline around one of the large end curves. Use ½″ No. 19 wire nails, one every four inches or so. The beveled edges of the cork strip represent the sloping ballast contour on prototype railroad track, and the sound-deadening effect of the cork helps your railroad run more quietly.

Start the second half strip on the other side of the curve centerline, with its end at the middle of the first piece. This overlapping ensures smooth curves and good appearance. At turnouts, continue the cork strips along the outside of the centerlines, then go back and cut pieces to fill in the middle areas. Use a sharp hobby knife to cut the cork at an angle for smooth joints. Temporarily position the turnouts and add scraps of cork strip under the actuating mechanisms to support them.

When all the cork is nailed in place, wrap medium-grit sandpaper around a wood block and use it to smooth the top surface of the roadbed. Don't remove much material, just knock off the high spots and irregularities that could interfere with level track placement.

Take your pick: "plain" or "fancy" wiring

Before fastening the track sections in place, decide whether you want to follow the "fancy" wiring scheme, fig. 2, or the "plain" wiring which involves only two wires running from the power pack to the track. The two wires energize all track sections any time the speed control is moved. The Snap-Switches are

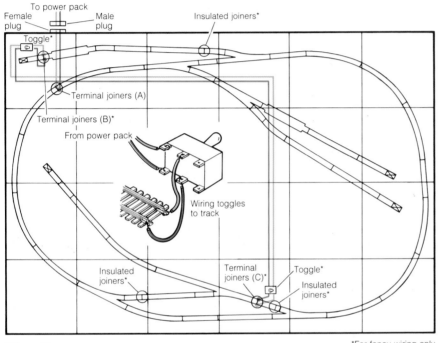

Fig. 2 WIRING DIAGRAM

*For fancy wiring only

The lettering on the YC engine and caboose was made using HO decal words available from Champion Decal Co., Minot, N. Dak. "Yule" was made by combining YUkon and yaLE; "Central," "Railway," and "Company" are "stock" decal words.

Sawhorses are one of many ways to support the Yule Central. Here benchwork is complete and the Snap-Track sections have been assembled and positioned properly on the tabletop. We placed bumper sections on each spur later, during final tracklaying.

When you have all track in place, mark the centerlines with a felt-tip pen, and make notes on the tabletop showing where to replace the track sections after the roadbed strips are added.

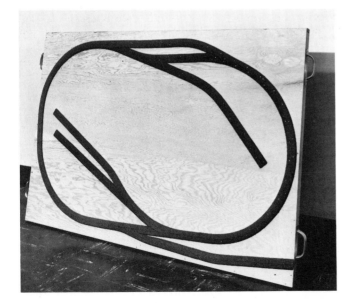

After your second evening of work, the Yule Central should look like this. The platform is complete, and all cork roadbed is fastened in place. Next: wiring and tracklaying.

TRACK AND WIRING COMPONENTS

Track parts

NOTE: This is a listing of all materials needed. If track and wiring items were supplied with your train set, subtract them from the quantities. All track in our list is Atlas Snap-Track; most standard HO train set track sizes are identical.

13	18″ radius full sections
2	18″ radius half sections
3	18″ radius third sections (one is usually provided with each turnout. If your turnouts include them, no additional sections are needed)
8	9″ straights
5	6″ straights
7	3″ straights
2	9″ straight rerailers
2	left-hand manual Snap-Switches
4	right-hand manual Snap-Switches
4	bumper sections
1	Snap-Track assortment (provides "fitter" sections)
12	HO cork roadbed strips
1 box	Atlas No. 2540 track nails
1 box	½″ No. 19 flathead wire nails
1	"Bright Boy" abrasive track cleaning block

medium-grit sandpaper

Wiring

"plain" wiring—1 set terminal rail joiners and 1 HO power pack

"fancy" wiring—the above, plus:

2 sets	terminal rail joiners
1 spool	18 AWG two-conductor insulated wire
2	subminiature double-pole, double-throw (dp.dt.) toggle switches (GC Electronics No. 35-010, Archer/Radio Shack No. 275-614, or equivalent)
2	plastic toggle covers to fit handles of above switches
1	4-pin chassis-mounted female cord connector receptacle (Calectro No. F3-264 or equivalent)
1	4-pin male cord connector (Calectro No. F3-244 or equivalent to match the female connector you have)
1	4-conductor retractile cable (Belden No. 8491 or equivalent)
4	spade-end wire terminals
1 pkg.	insulated rail joiners

resin-core solder

2-part 5-minute-setting epoxy adhesive

Tools required: Screwdriver, hammer, nail set, fine-point felt-tip pen, hobby knife, ³/₃₂″ and ¹/₄″ twist drill bits*, hand or power drill*, soldering iron or gun*, small needle files, needle-nose pliers, wire stripping pliers*, staple gun* (*these items required only for "fancy" wiring)

Above: The "dust" on the Yule hardware store is powdered chalk; otherwise, the structure is a simple plastic kit dressed up with paint and decals.

Left: The Dry Gulch Mine is one of two "kitbashed" (modified) buildings. It was converted from coaling tower to ore tipple by removing the coal hoist shed and the hoist machinery from the upper portion of the structure.

Above: This helicopter view of Yule's Main Street shows how the railroad tracks appear to be tucked between the buildings, roads, and scenic features, instead of vice versa.

Above: The Trailblazer Hotel is a fixture on Railroad Avenue. The yellow lines in the road were made by spraying paint through a narrow slot cut in a 3 x 5 index card.

Above: Goldie's Place is only one of several businesses in this ramshackle masonry structure. Compare the other photos carefully, and you'll find signs for six different tenants!

Above: Looking west into town from the Main Street grade crossing — The YC's caboose is rattling over the crossing to the right, the dry creek bed behind the gas station is in the center, and the town lies to the left.

Right: The abbreviated yard at Yule is located just off Railroad Avenue. The far spur is the company siding, and the closer siding serves the lumber dealer.

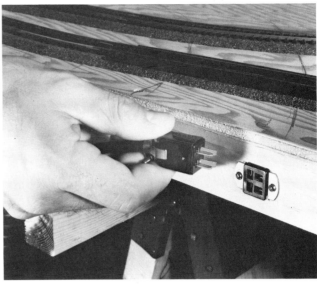

One of our "fancy" tabletop toggle switches — this one energizes the Dry Gulch passing siding and mine spur tracks. The switch is epoxied in place from beneath — an installation method that proved permanent and trouble-free. Note the terminal joiners and feeders to the left of the toggle, and the light-colored insulating joiners to the right.

The plug connector for the power pack is located at the front of the layout near the interchange siding. We use only two of the conductors in this four-conductor plug for our "fancy" wiring scheme, but we'll put the other wires to work when we improve the layout with a tethered throttle such as the hand-held unit shown on page 24.

designed and constructed so gaps, jumpers, or other wires aren't required.

The "fancy" wiring scheme isn't really fancy at all. It requires only two additional sets of track feeders, three pairs of insulated rail joiners, and a couple subminiature toggle switches. The toggles allow you to turn off the power to two sections of the layout — the interchange track and the passing siding and mine spur — so you can leave an engine or short train at either place while operating another train on the main line. This is not true two-train operation (that requires two power packs), but you can have more than one locomotive on the layout at once — something you can't do with the plain wiring unless you are satisfied to run both locomotives in the same direction at the same time. The only disadvantage of the "fancy" scheme is that it requires soldering, but this is a skill you'll want to acquire anyway.

Putting the track down for good

Having chosen your wiring scheme, assemble the track sections on top of the roadbed and install the terminal and insulated rail joiners where they are required. The optional terminal joiner and insulated joiner locations for the "fancy" setup are designated by asterisks (*) in the figures. Once again, go over the track twice, pushing the sections together and making sure there are no wide gaps or misalignments at the joints. Check carefully to see that none of the rail joiners are spread, bent, or distorted; if you find defective joiners, replace them using the spares furnished with the track fitter assortment.

When the track is adjusted and

aligned over the cord roadbed, start pushing track nails through the holes in the ties and into the roadbed with needle-nose pliers. You will note that the Snap-Switches don't have holes for nails. Why? Because the Snap-Switches are meant to be anchored by the adjoining track sections, leaving the turnout free to "float" in the best position for smooth operation.

Work your way around the layout placing two nails in each track section, and follow up with a light hammer tap — light enough only to seat the nails in the plywood. Then place nails in all the remaining holes and give them the same light tap.

Now place the broad end of your nail set on top of the track nails and tap them into the plywood with a succession of light blows. Don't drive the nails completely home because there must be a little "breathing space" between the top of the tie and the bottom of the nail head. If the nail head contacts the top of the tie it can bend the track, narrowing the gauge and causing derailments, so it is better to err on the "loose" side here. When you have all the track nailed down, go over the layout once more to check that each rail joiner spans its joint equally. If not, use the needle-nose pliers or the point of the nail set to gently slide the joiner so half of it is on each side of the joint.

Plugs, wires, and tabletop toggles

Drill $3/32''$ holes through the plywood top and lead a wire from each terminal joiner through to the underside of the layout. For the plain wiring you can either lead these directly to the variable d.c. terminals on your power pack (via a

$1/4''$ hole in the side of the layout platform frame) or install a convenient plug-and-receptacle arrangement as in the "fancy" wiring scheme.

Perhaps the biggest advantage of the fancy wiring setup on the Yule Central is that it does *not* require building a control panel. With the isolation toggles for the siding and spurs built into the tabletop, the whole layout becomes the control panel. Drill $1/4''$ holes through the plywood for the toggle switches, cut a hole in the side of the layout for the female plug socket (fig. 3), and make temporary connections to toggles, track feeders, and power pack to test your wiring. If a locomotive runs in the direction opposite to the main line on one of the spurs controlled by a toggle, reverse the leads from that toggle to the track. When everything operates satisfactorily, solder the connections and install the plug receptacle in the side of the benchwork. Rather than add the clutter

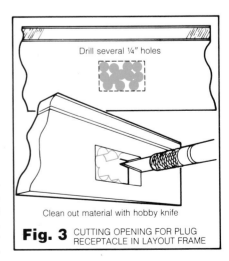

Drill several ¼" holes

Clean out material with hobby knife

Fig. 3 CUTTING OPENING FOR PLUG RECEPTACLE IN LAYOUT FRAME

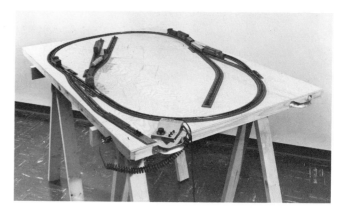

In less than a week of evenings your YC should look like this. With the wiring completed and the trackwork fastened down permanently, the pike is ready for the Christmas tree — if that's what you have in mind — or for scenery. The power pack, shown here perched on the corner of the layout, is best placed on a small table or the seat of a chair during operation.

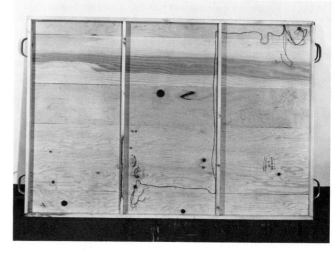

Here's an action meet on the Yule Central: A borrowed Cotton Belt GP40 is "in the hole" on the Dry Gulch mine spur with a short freight while a Southern Pacific F7 growls past with a two-car excursion train. The realistic weeds in the foreground are made by pushing short bits of yarn into scenery with sharp-pointed tweezers. The "antelopes" are N scale deer.

This flip-side view shows the Yule Central in the same stage of completion as the upper photo. The wires run from the plug receptacle to the two tabletop toggle switches and the three terminal joiner locations. Note how the wires are routed *through* the crossmember and stapled to the plywood to prevent snagging when the layout is moved.

of mounting hardware, I used a two-part 5-minute-setting epoxy adhesive to fasten the toggle in place from the bottom of the layout. Use lots of the glue for strength, but be careful to keep it out of the toggle lever area.

I stapled the wires to the bottom of the plywood to keep them from hanging down and snagging on things when the layout is moved. I also drilled a ¼" hole through one of the crossmembers for the wires leading to the passing siding and mine spur, so the layout can be set on a flat surface without fear of pinching the wires. To disguise the shiny silver toggle levers, cover them with the small plastic covers available for that purpose.

Testing and troubleshooting

Your Yule Central should run smoothly the first time you crack the throttle, but we've still got some testing to do and a few refinements to make. Go

over the rails with your fingers, feeling for uneven joints, misalignments, and other irregularities. Run the train, noting all places where the cars bump or rock. Determine the cause and use a small file to smooth out the offending area. See the box on "Rail joints and switch points" in the Marquette & Independence story and work over your track as explained there. Be fussy — this work may not be much fun, but it greatly increases the fun of operating your layout later.

With the trackwork down, wiring completed, and the layout tested and tuned, the Yule Central is ready for use as an operating display. If you aren't planning to add scenery right away but want to improve on the bare wood look of the layout, paint the platform top and edges with a coat of the golden tan color latex paint listed in the scenery materials. If you're still raring to go, let's forge ahead with some scenery —

and some personality — for the Yule Central.

Personality for the YC

My version of the Yule Central is an example of a model railroad built with a specific theme in mind. The pike represents a present-day Arizona or New Mexico shortline railroad that connects with the Southern Pacific. The little outfit doesn't go very far or very fast with its mixture of cast-off and hand-me-down SP equipment. It's main job is to serve the run-down, dusty little town of Yule (pronounced *you-lee*) and the small mining operation nearby. Choosing such a theme is valuable on any model railroad because it establishes a framework into which everything must fit — or nearly so — and many modelers find that choosing what elements to include or leave out ranks as one of the most enjoyable and challenging aspects of the hobby.

The photos of the completed Yule Central show how you can carry out the Southwestern theme. For reference, I browsed through an encyclopedia and an Arizona travel magazine to look at the forms and colors of the scenery. Regardless of the theme or locale you choose, this is a valuable step; even if you want to model your own back yard, take the time to step outdoors and look —really *look*– at the real thing.

You can follow any one of several avenues of attack in building scenery. You can build the structures first, placing them on the layout to see how they will "fit" and how roads, hills, and so on will form around them, or you can rough out the scenery forms first and choose structures and details that will fit the space left for them. I chose the latter method. Although I started out by doodling roads, structure locations, and scenery outlines on the plywood, I found that these early ideas changed as the scenery was built and added to the layout.

The central ridge divider

Any scenery makes a model railroad seem bigger, and on the Yule Central we're going to use a trick that dramatically expands the layout: a high central ridge running diagonally across the table top. This ridge effectively divides the layout into two viewing areas, and because it can hide a six- or seven-car freight train from the viewer during half the trip around the layout, the main line seems longer.

The ridge brings several other advantages. First, because there is a sharp break between the two scenes, you can make them different from each other without incongruity. This makes the layout more interesting because the train appears to go from one scene to the other, and the distance between them can be as far as your imagination will allow. I tried to achieve a parched, dry look on the side with the mine, but I made the scenery greener and more habitable on the town side. Equally important, you can develop your scenic skills while working on the "back" of the layout, then take on the "front" when you have a good handle on the techniques and materials. Later, you can change one side of the ridge, but you'll always have one area completed for viewing. Finally, with a little ingenuity you could make the central ridge removable so the railroad can accommodate the Christmas tree year after year.

Featherweight scenery without plaster

Most model railroad scenery is made with plaster—see the Bantam & Cycloid and Marquette & Independence stories for plasterworking techniques—but I chose extruded sheet Styrofoam insulating material to make the basic contours of the bluffs and other

EQUIPMENT FOR THE YULE CENTRAL

THE enormous variety of equipment offered in HO is one of that scale's greatest selling points. Here are six trains that are very much at home on the Yule Central. Some of the cars are ready-to-run items, the rest are easy-to-assemble plastic kits that require no special skills and go together in less than an hour. All of the locomotives are ready-to-run. Generally, short engines and short cars will operate more smoothly on the Yule Central's 18"-radius curves, allow more cars per train and more flexibility in switching, and make the layout look bigger than will longer rolling stock. You'll find diesels in five out of six cases because in general they are less expensive and more trouble-free in operation for beginners, and less delicate. Each of the locomotives and cars is available in a variety of railroad names and markings so you can choose railroads to correspond to your geographical area or the theme you choose for your version of the YC.

There's no requirement to start with a train set — you can assemble your own!

Athearn EMD SW1500 diesel switcher, Athearn 40-foot pulpwood car, Athearn 40-foot hy-cube ("ugly duckling") box car, Train Miniature 40-foot X-29 steel box car, Athearn wide-vision caboose.

Atlas EMD GP40 road-switcher, Athearn 50-foot covered gondola, Athearn 34-foot ribbed-side twin hopper, Athearn 50-foot mechanical refrigerator, Athearn steel caboose (this equipment came in our Atlas train set, but it is all available separately).

AHM 0-8-0 steam switcher with tender, Train Miniature 40-foot steel ice-bunker refrigerator, Model Die Casting (Roundhouse) 34-foot covered hopper, Athearn 40-foot single-dome tank car, Model Die Casting outside-braced wood caboose.

Athearn EMD F7A road diesel, Model Die Casting 60-foot Harriman combine and 60-foot Harriman coach.

AHM Alco-GE 1000-h.p. diesel switcher, Train Miniature 40-foot outside-braced wood box car, AHM 60-foot double-door box car, Athearn 40-foot grain-loading box car, Athearn bay window caboose.

Atlas EMD GP40 road diesel, Model Die Casting 40-foot steel box car, Athearn 40-foot single-dome tank car, Athearn 40-foot flat car, Model Die Casting 60-foot Harriman combine.

SCENERY MATERIALS

2 sheets	2' x 8' x 1"-thick extruded Styrofoam insulation
1 pt.	water-soluble contact adhesive (Elmer's No. E461 Cabinetmaker's Contact Cement, Weldwood "Plus-10", Weldwood "Home Safe", or equivalent)
1 qt.	flat interior latex paint, custom-mixed to match Polly S PR83 "Mud" (Sears Custom Color No. 860, Kyanize Color Spree No. 5-12D "Tijuana", or other color match)
1 qt.	acrylic polymer matte medium (Liquitex, Grumbacher, Utrecht Linen, or equivalent)
1 pkg.	scenery modeling compound (Perma-Scene or Sculptamold)
8 oz.	acrylic latex spackling compound (Elmer's Redi-Spack or equivalent)
1 btl.	John's Lab "Better Wetter" wetting agent
1 bag ea.	John's Lab "Grass" (flock), No. 402 green, No. 405 gold, No. 406 beige, No. 407 rust
1 btl. ea.	Polly S water-soluble railroad colors, PR13 Grimy Black, PR30 Reefer Orange
3 bags	Campbell Scale Models blended ballast No. 790 light gray
1 bag	Campbell blended ballast No. 793 decomposed granite
1 box	Campbell lichen No. 604 gray
2 kits	Woodland Scenics trees No. TK-16 3¼" wide spread
1 box	AHM See-niks trees No. 3710K maple
1 bag ea.	Woodland Scenics turf No. T-50 earth, No. T-64 medium green
2 pkgs. ea.	MLR Products sand No. SM-5101 fine, No. SM-5112 coarse
1 pkg.	MLR Products large rough rocks No. SM-5104
1	4 oz. spray can flat roof brown enamel

white glue
1" masking tape
scraps of doublewall corrugated cardboard
scraps of green, gold, and brown yarn

Tools required: Household pump sprayer bottle, eyedropper, 2" brush, No. 2 flat watercolor brush, wood rasp and Surform tools, sieve (strainer), large palette knife, plastic mixing bowl, plastic spatula, sharp-pointed tweezers, plastic drop cloth, disposable plastic cups and holder, assorted empty bottles, cans, and jars, screwdriver, hand keyhole or power saber saw, vacuum cleaner

The scenicked layout will look like this before you add structures — interesting, but desolate. Note how effectively the high central ridge divides the layout into two distinct viewing areas. These viewing areas are like "stages" where the "actors" (our trains) enter and exit from the "wings." With just a little ingenuity you could easily mount the central ridge from under the tabletop, making the ridge removable to make room for the Christmas tree year after year.

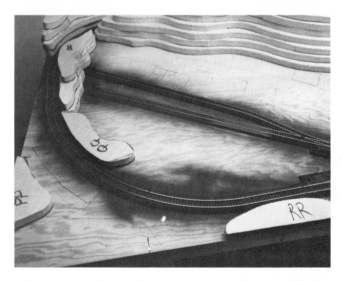

A light spray coating of dark brown enamel effectively kills the plastic shine on your sectional track and vastly improves the realism of your finished trackwork. This view also shows how the Styrofoam scenery wafers are stacked.

features around Yule. This material is cut and stacked like the layers of a cake, then glued together and formed with a coarse wood rasp and various shapes of Surform tools. Styrofoam is light (a good selling point for a portable layout), strong, and resilient.

The greatest advantages of Styrofoam over plaster are its inherent cleanliness and the leisurely manner in which it can be worked. Plaster scenery requires working with a batterlike liquid that sets whether you're ready or not. With Styrofoam, if the phone or doorbell rings, you simply put down your rasp or paint brush and come back later, with no lost motion or material. Plaster powder has a way of getting into clothes, flooring, and trackwork. Styrofoam shaping operations generate only a dry, light sawdustlike debris that vacuums up easily. Generally, operations that require liquids are performed *off* the layout, so you can accomplish the messy work out-of-doors or in the garage or cellar and bring the completed, *dry*, scenery pieces to the layout.

First—a spray can full of track realism

Before we launch into scenery-forming, coloring, and texturing, let's take a few moments to improve the appearance of our sectional trackwork. *Lightly* spray the rails, ties, and turnout actuator housings with an aerosol can of flat roof-brown enamel (enamel won't damage the plastic parts.) The paint covers the unrealistic glossy black ties and shiny rail, makes the turnout actuators less conspicuous, and brings out the wood grain detail in the ties. Immediately after painting, go over the tops and inside edges of the rails with an abrasive track-cleaning block, and run an engine with metal wheels over the trackwork to remove all traces of paint from the electrical contact surfaces. The locomotive wheels will pick up paint from the track, so you'll have to scrape the tread and flange surfaces with a sharp wooden stick to remove the residue. Work the turnouts back and forth several times to ensure that the paint doesn't jam them.

Styrofoam cutting and forming

Purchase Styrofoam sheets at a lumber yard, or check your Yellow Pages for listings under "Insulation Materials." Be sure to specify *extruded* Styrofoam. Draw grid lines spaced six inches apart on your Styrofoam panels, and transfer the patterns for the parts from fig. 5 to this grid. Label the parts and cut them out with a power saber saw or hand keyhole saw. The fine dust from the sawing operations may irritate your nose, so consider wearing a dust mask. If you can, work outdoors, but if you work inside have a vacuum cleaner on hand to whisk up the debris so it doesn't get tracked all over. Dust off the pieces and stack them on the layout as shown in fig. 6 and the photos. If the pieces seem too large don't worry—they'll "shrink" when we form rounded and sloping contours.

Now remove the bottom four wafers from each stack and glue them together with water-soluble contact cement. Follow the instructions that come with the adhesive. To simulate bands of rock that have eroded less readily than the softer material above and below them, we will work on layers one through four and five and above as separate units, joining them *after* shaping.

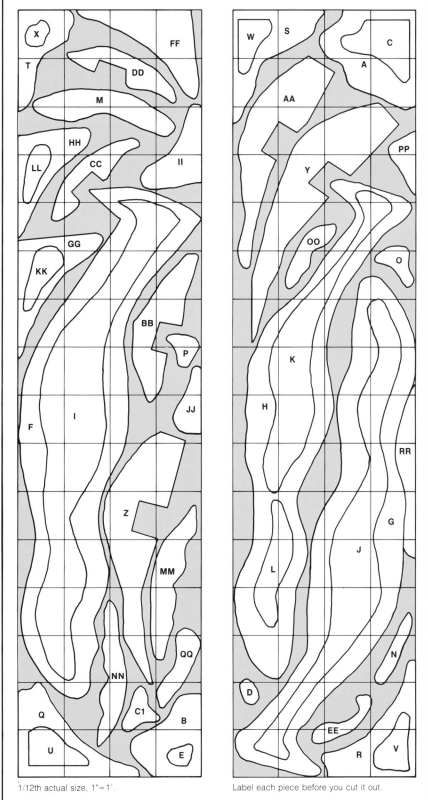

1/12th actual size, 1″=1′.

Label each piece before you cut it out.

Divide two 2′ x 8′ sheets of 1″ extruded Styrofoam into 6″ squares and transfer the patterns with a felt marking pen. Work with one square at a time, drawing the pattern lines through the squares on the Styrofoam the same way they go through the squares on the figure, just as dressmaking patterns are enlarged.

Fig. 5 STYROFOAM CUTTING PATTERNS

Use the rasp and Surform tools to round and slope the stacked units as shown in the photo sequence. Check the units occasionally to see how they fit on the layout, and run a train made up of your longest locomotives and cars to check clearances around the scenery contours. Remember to leave a flat gluing surface where the upper and lower units will meet, and keep in mind that the edges of layers five and six represent harder rock and should remain more or less vertical compared to the sloping contours of the other parts. When you are satisfied with the overall shapes, glue the upper and lower units together and crumble the edges of layers five and six with a screwdriver tip to simulate eroded rock faces. Before adding color and texture, check the pieces for fit on the layout once more and cut away any areas that interfere with the passage of the trains.

Mud, sand, and sparse vegetation

To color our scenery the golden tan of the sandy Southwest, we're going to forsake such exotic media as artists' colors in tubes and use ordinary household latex flat interior wall paint. Most paint and hardware stores have a custom color mixing machine, and if you bring a dried sample of Polly S PR83 "Mud," the store will be able to match it to a color in the mixing machine catalog. When you have the paint at home, mix some of it with equal parts of water in a resealable

wide-mouth jar. This diluted paint will serve not only as our basic color, but also as an adhesive.

Cover your working surface with several layers of newspaper—this project

can be messy. Brush diluted paint on one of the formed Styrofoam scenery pieces, working it into the surface thoroughly. While the paint is wet, sprinkle coarse sand over it as shown in

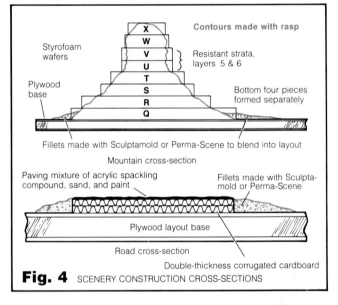

Fig. 6 STYROFOAM STACKING KEY

When you've cut all the Styrofoam wafers and stacked them on the layout, your Yule Central should look like this. Check to see that there is adequate clearance for your trains, then glue together layers 1-4 and 5 and above.

Fig. 4 SCENERY CONSTRUCTION CROSS-SECTIONS

These are the tools you'll need to contour your Styrofoam scenery. Left to right: Power drill with rotary Surform tools (optional), coarse wood rasp, Surform planes. The power drill speeds the work, but cleanup takes longer because the mess is spread farther.

To achieve the effect of resistant rock strata, contour the bottom four layers of each scenery stack separately. Vacuum up the coarse Styrofoam debris after each forming session, otherwise, it tends to get tracked everywhere.

Once the top and bottom sections of a scenery stack are formed and glued together you can simulate crumbling rock faces by gouging the foam with the tip of a large screwdriver blade. It's easy, and you'll find the result is just as effective as laborious rock carving.

Flat interior latex wall paint provides both coloration and adhesive in this scenery technique. First, brush a liberal coat of thinned paint all over one formed Styrofoam scenery chunk. Work the paint into the surface thoroughly with the brush.

Next, sprinkle coarse sand into the wet paint to add realistic texture. The plastic coffee cup holder shown in the background is very handy for scenery work; the disposable inserts are inexpensive and using them saves a lot of cleanup time.

A slightly different color helps to emphasize the eroded rock strata of layers 5 and 6. While the base color is still wet, brush diluted orange or red Polly S onto the rock area, and let it blend in and run down the slope realistically.

the photo sequence. The paint will surround the sand particles, coloring and bonding them in place.

To add a subtly different color to the rocky strata of layers five and six, dip your brush into a cup containing thinned orange or bright red Polly S paint, and dab this over the rocky strata while the base color is still wet. The brighter color will blend together with the mud base and produce realistic mottling. Also, some of the second color will trickle down the slope, producing the effect of sediments washed from the rocky layer.

Now mix a solution of one part acrylic matte medium and three parts water, with a few drops of wetting agent, liquid dish detergent, or Kodak Photo-Flo per pint to make the solution flow better. Use a pump sprayer bottle to mist this bonding solution over the scenery chunk. Spray the matte medium on the scenery until the surface is moist, but stop short of washing away the sand and paint. The matte medium solution acts as a bonding and sealing agent for the sand and flock texture materials, firmly fixing them to the scenery.

Dispense two or three colors of flock "grass" into your sieve and dust them over the glistening wet scenery chunk. The flock will miss the vertical surfaces and fall on the gentle slopes. Don't use much green—a little goes a long way —and always combine at least two colors in the sieve to achieve realistic color gradations. When you are satisfied with the effect, mist on just a little more matte medium and sprinkle coarse ground foam rubber here and there to represent splotchy vegetation. Don't overdo this last step or you will undo the harsh, bare look we've created.

As you finish coloring and texturing each scenery chunk, set it aside on newspapers to dry overnight. By morning, the pieces will be dry. Position them on the layout and check once more for adequate clearance. When everything fits, use white glue to attach the scenery pieces to the plywood base and give them overnight to set before continuing.

Roads and structure bases

If we place roads and structures directly on the plywood table top they will be too low in relation to the track, so we must add a base to bring them up to a more realistic height. I used one thickness of double-wall corrugated cardboard (two layers of standard corrugated stock will also work). Cut this material to the approximate outlines shown in fig. 7 and glue it in place with the contact adhesive. I also drove a few staples through the cardboard where they would be covered by the structures.

Our next job is to blend the Styrofoam scenery, cardboard road and structure bases, and the flat plywood layout platform so there are no abrupt changes in contour. To do this, we'll use a commercial scenery modeling compound; two such products are listed in the bill of materials. These products are clean to work with, have longer working times than plaster mixes, and dry to a light, resilient material. Of the two, Perma-Scene has the longer working time, but also a much longer setting time.

Mix small batches of the modeling compound and apply them as blending fillets around the Styrofoam sections and road bases. My favorite tool here is the long-handled palette knife shown in the photos. When you have the larger forms blended, add small knolls with the modeling compound to any areas that look too flat.

When the modeling compound dries, paint over it with diluted latex mud color, and add sand and grass textures with the bonding solution just as you did on the Styrofoam pieces. Be careful to keep the matte medium solution away from the moving parts of the toggles and turnouts; it is an effective glue.

Road paving and scenic details

To simulate blacktop road paving material, mix equal parts of acrylic spackling compound and fine sand with enough Polly S PR13 "Grimy Black" paint to make a medium-gray color.

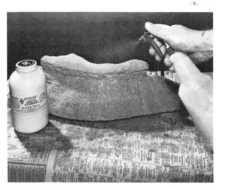

Lightly mist the scenery chunk with diluted acrylic matte medium until the surface glistens. This spray helps blend the colors and acts as the bonding agent to bind the paint, sand, Styrofoam, and flock into a rugged, resilient scenic skin.

Before the matte medium has a chance to dry, dust the flock "grass" with a fine strainer. The "grass" will miss the vertical rock surfaces, leaving them devoid of vegetation. Keep at least two colors of flock in the sieve, and beware of too much green.

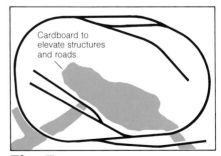

Cardboard to elevate structures and roads

Fig. 7 ROAD AND STRUCTURE BASES

SUGGESTED STRUCTURES

	NOTE: All structures are plastic kits.
2	Atlas No. 707 station platforms (each kit contains two platforms, three are needed to build the station at Yule)
1	Atlas No. 705 telephone shanty and pole
1	Atlas No. 775 telephone poles (optional)
1	Atlas No. 750 lumber yard and office
1	AHM No. 5851 trackside structures set
1	AHM No. 5878 Busy Bee department store
1	AHM No. 5833 coaling tower (for ore tipple)
1	Model Die Casting No. 506 street scene
1	Model Die Casting No. 3067 36-foot old-time boxcar (for storage shed)
1 ea.	Micro-Scale decal sets No. 87-162 rural farming community signs, No. 87-163 small rural town signs
	masking tape

Tools required: Liquid plastic cement, decal setting solvent, plastic-compatible paint set, pastel chalk sticks, small files, 1/2"-wide flat lettering brush, No. 4 flat oil-color brush, hobby knife and spare blades, tweezers

After you complete each piece of scenery and allow it to dry overnight, place it on the layout and check once again for adequate clearance for your trains, then glue it in place with white glue. After another overnight setting period for the glue, start blending the contours into the layout with modeling compound.

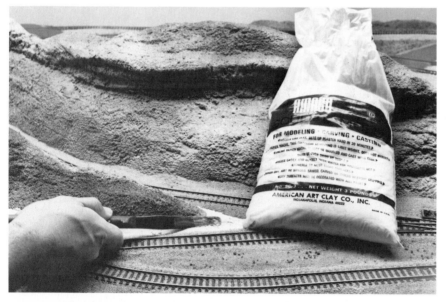

A palette knife is a handy tool for working modeling compound into the gaps between the Styrofoam scenery chunks and the plywood tabletop. Here the track is already ballasted, but most of the scenery was in place *before* track ballasting.

Moisten the surface of your road base with a mist of diluted matte medium bonding solution and apply the paving mixture with a palette or putty knife. Spread the mixture so it covers the cardboard support, overlaps the modeling compound fillets, and runs up to the rails at the road crossings. At the three road crossings that don't coincide with rerailer locations, trowel paving mixture between the rails and clear the flangeways with your modeling knife. Run a car through each crossing several times to make sure the flangeways are unobstructed, then clean the wheels with water and a cotton swab.

I scattered a handful of small pebbles in the area between the town structures and the central ridge to represent a dry creek bed, and dropped more stones into the steep cuts at the corners of the layout to represent rocks that had broken off and rolled down to trackside. All rocks were bonded in place with diluted matte medium. I spent one evening touching up ragged edges with thinned latex paint and adding sand and ground foam texture material to give an overall finished look to the layout.

Ballast holds it all together

Most modelers ballast their trackwork soon after putting it down, and their methods work fine. My preference is to save this step for last and use the ballast to cover the rough edges of the scenery along the track. Start by spreading ballast between the ties and outside the rails along the sloping roadbed contour. Be *very* careful to keep ballast particles out of the moving parts of the turnouts and actuators. Use a soft-bristled brush to move the ballast around and take as much time as you need to get it exactly where you want it—there's no changing the distribution of the material once you commence the bonding process.

For a ballast bonding agent we'll use the same mixture of matte medium, water, and wetting agent that we used

In this low-flying airplane view of downtown Yule, note how the trees have been kept close to the buildings. This helps separate the structures from the scenery, enhancing the feeling of "wide-open spaces."

to bond the texture materials in place on the rest of the layout. Start by misting a one-foot section of ballasted trackwork with a solution of water and wetting agent. Let this saturate the ballast particles. Now dribble the matte medium bonding solution into the wetted ballast with an eyedropper. Again, be very sparing with the matte medium around the turnouts, and be sure *none* of it finds its way into the moving parts, but use lots of bonding agent on the other parts of the track. When the bonding agent dries, the ballast particles will be firmly affixed, but will look loose.

Structures, trees, and some details

By now, your Yule Central should look complete even without structures. The list of suggested structures is intended only to tell you what I used, because you probably have some ideas of your own. Most of the structures are small—it's more interesting to have

Top: The plastic base for the lumber shed formed an integral part of the structure and could not be discarded as were the bases for the other buildings. After trimming back the base as much as possible, the edges were disguised with sand. Bottom: The supply shed on the railroad company spur track is a recycled old-time wood box car.

five or six small buildings than one or two sprawling ones—and they go together to form a convincing semi-ghost town. Today's plastic structure kits are easy-to-build, well-proportioned, and highly detailed. With care in painting and assembly they rival scratchbuilt models.

Rather than assembling all the structures at once, I suggest you go about this aspect of construction piecemeal, alternating structures with car kits, layout work, and other projects. The biggest single improvement you can make to any plastic model is to paint it with flat colors to mask the plastic sheen and bring out the detail, so paint all parts with plastic-compatible paint before assembly—there are several types, including flat colors made for military

models as well as those made specifically for the model railroad field.

When you have completed a structure, "weather" it by dusting on pastel chalk powder (made by rubbing chalk sticks on sandpaper). I glued each structure to the layout with white glue, and worked sand, flock, ground foam, and other texture materials around the bases to hide gaps between the walls and the "ground" surface. This easy finishing step is important: Gaping cracks between the buildings and the ground can destroy all the realism you've worked so hard to achieve.

I assembled trees from the kits listed in the scenery bill of materials and grouped them behind the town buildings in the dry creek bed. Small tufts of gray lichen "planted" with white glue

represent scrub growth and tumbleweed, and the briar patch behind the gas station was made by chopping up coarse lichen pieces with scissors, spraying with matte medium bonding solution, and sprinkling on ground foam-rubber "turf."

Even a small layout can absorb a great deal of detail, and it's up to you where to draw the line with your Yule Central. I added a few vehicles, figures, old tires, trash cans, discarded scrap, shipping pallets, and other details. One of the most enjoyable aspects of completing a layout is adding more and more detail to it as time goes by, and you'll find that the more you add, the more interesting the layout becomes, both to you and to those who view and operate it with you.

KADEE COUPLERS

IMPROVEMENTS FOR THE YULE CENTRAL

UNLIKE projects in many other hobbies, a model railroad — even a small one like our Yule Central — rarely, if ever, is finished. With the addition of scenery, structures, and details the YC is "complete," but there are still plenty of things to do — small improvements and short mini-projects that will boost your enjoyment of the layout and open doors to more facets of scale model railroading.

No other improvement will upgrade the operating quality of the layout as much as adding the Kadee brand coupling and uncoupling system. This means converting locomotives and rolling stock to Kadee magnetic couplers, and placing Kadee uncoupling ramps in the spur tracks and interchange siding. Neither task takes long to accomplish. Your cars will couple more easily and back up better, and the reliable automatic uncoupling feature makes switching much more fun than with the horn-hook couplers. GH Products makes a hand-held uncoupling tool to separate cars on the main line or at other locations where you don't have a ramp.

My next improvement was a tethered, add-on throttle unit. This control box is mounted on a long cord, and is designed to be held in the hand. It allows you to move around the layout with the train. Ours draws its power from the original pack we bought with the train set, and uses all four leads in the plug receptacle (fig. 3) to route power to and from the hand-held unit. Installation was easy, and there are several brands available.

Once you get the hang of switching and buy or build additional cars, you'll need a place to store the overflow rolling stock. With only a few evenings' work and a little material, you can build an add-on yard section to connect with the Yule interchange siding. Kalmbach's HO RAILROAD THAT GROWS shows how to construct a hinged, drop-leaf yard, and you could adapt that design or build a permanent wall shelf at the correct height to coincide with the layout. Fig. 8 is a suggested track plan for a 24" x 48" storage yard. By now you've mastered the skills of platform construction, roadbed- and tracklaying, and scenery work that you'll need for the yard area, so you're on your own for this improvement.

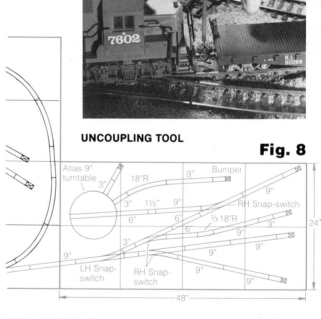

UNCOUPLING TOOL

Fig. 8

Atlas 9" turntable

18"R   Bumper

3"   1½"   9"   RH Snap-switch

6"   6"   ⅓ 18"R

6"   3"

LH Snap-switch   RH Snap-switch

9"

—48"—   —24"—

HAND-HELD THROTTLE

UNCOUPLING RAMPS

This N scale pike proves no space is too small

Tunnels, hills, buildings, a spur—all in 2x4

Zip-textured scenery—just like the big layouts

Two-train operation with dual cab control

Store it in a closet or under a bed

Building the Bantam & Cycloid Railroad

BY WALT OLSEN

I HAVE always felt that anyone who really wants a layout can have one regardless of his space limitations. When a friend of mine who lives in a very small New York apartment insisted he was the exception, I took it as a challenge and decided to build an N scale layout for him that he could easily store in a closet or under a bed when not in use. The result of the self-imposed challenge was the Bantam & Cycloid Railroad, a scant 18½" x 33" pike with a built-in power supply and control panel.

A layout as small as this is practical for any location where space is at an absolute premium, such as a college dormitory, military barracks, or mobile home. Also, if you're a beginner, building a small layout like the B&C is a good

way to learn about model railroad construction without investing a lot of money or spending a great deal of time on any single step.

When I designed this layout I wanted more than a simple oval. For operating interest the track plan offers several routing choices for mainline trains, and even allows you to operate two trains.

I planned my layout, fig. 1, intending to use Atlas flexible track and a minimum radius of 7". I used Minitrix switches, which have a 7½" radius through the curved portion, to save space. Because beginning modelers may prefer sectional track, I have included alternate drawings (figs. 2 and 3) for the layout using Minitrix and Rapido sectional track. Overall, these layouts are

larger because the sectional track radius is larger. Although the 7" radius for the fig. 1 plan is smaller than what is usually recommended for N scale, I found that most diesels, small steam engines, and standard-length freight cars negotiate the curves with ease.

Getting started

The first step in constructing the B&C is to build the frame and baseboard, fig. 4. The sizes depend on which variation of the track plan you choose. The parts can be cut to size at the lumber yard and carried home under your arm. The frame is 1 x 2 stock and the top is ¼" plywood; assembly is simply a matter of applying white glue to the joints and fastening the pieces together with screws or nails.

The next step is to draw the track plan on the plywood surface. If you are using sectional track, put the track together temporarily and trace around it. If you are using flexible track as I did, you'll have to lay out the track lines using a ruler and a compass or circle template. You can make your own circle template using heavy cardstock, or you can make a simple trammel radius tool, fig. 5.

Roadbed and track

Once the track plan is drawn on the baseboard, you are ready to install the cork roadbed. Using the marks on the plywood as a guide, fasten the cork to the baseboard with small nails or staples. I started the job using track nails, but I found the roadbed could be attached more quickly using a staple gun and ⅜" staples. If you use staples you may have to tap them down with a hammer to get them flush with the top of the cork.

Tracklaying comes next, but before you start, skip ahead and read the comments on wiring. Some of the preliminary wiring can be accomplished more easily while you lay the track.

Use ½" No. 20 wire brads to fasten the track to the cork roadbed. First locate both sets of turnouts, then add the track between them. If you are using flexible track, arrange the sections so that there are no joints on the curves. This can be done by placing short pieces of straight track between the curves. By not having joints on the curves, the derailment hazard is greatly reduced.

If you plan to run only one train at a time, all of the track can be fed from two wires from your power pack. You can solder these wires to the two rails (place the wires low on the outside so nothing protrudes above rail height to lift the locomotive and car wheels), but it would be easier to connect them to a standard terminal-track section.

Wiring for two train operation

To run two or more trains independently you'll need one power pack for each train you intend to operate, and

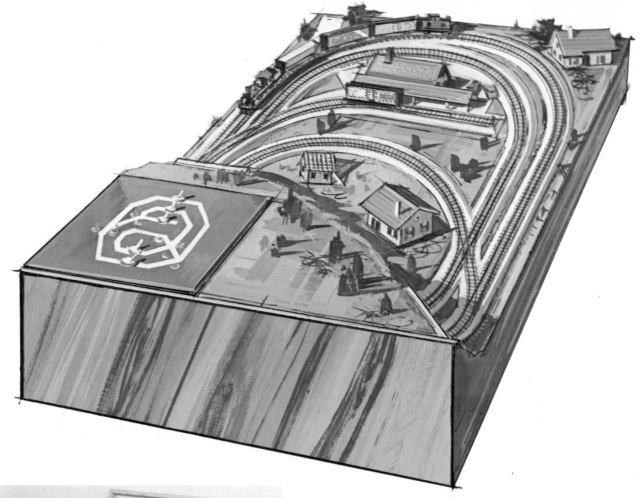

Above: The kitchen table is big enough to serve as work-space for the Bantam & Cycloid. Right: the finished railroad.

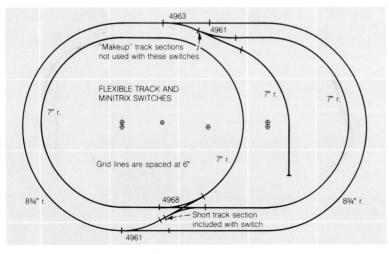

the track will have to be divided into separate electrical zones called "blocks." Each block is insulated from all others, and each has its own wires to the power packs through a selector switch that assigns a power pack to that block. This switch also has an off position so block power can be completely cut off. With this system of train control, trains can run or stop independently as

Fig. 1   TRACK REQUIRED

(1) Minitrix 4968 double-slip switch
(1) Minitrix 4963 right-hand switch
(2) Minitrix 4961 left-hand switch
(6) Atlas 2500 flex track
(1) Minitrix 4972 terminal track (optional)
(7) Atlas or Midwest Products cork roadbed
(1) Minitrix 6525 metal rail joiners

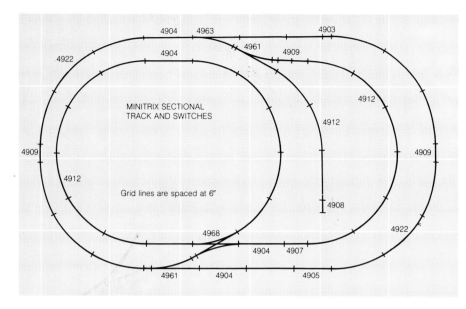

Fig. 2   TRACK REQUIRED (all Minitrix)

(1) 4968, (2) 4961, (1) 4963, (12) 4922, (19) 4912, (2) 4903, (8) 4904, (2) 4905, (1) 4907, (1) 4908, (4) 4909, (1) 4972 (optional), (7) Atlas or Midwest Products cork roadbed

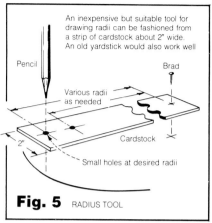

An inexpensive but suitable tool for drawing radii can be fashioned from a strip of cardstock about 2" wide. An old yardstick would also work well

Pencil

Brad

Various radii as needed

2"

Cardstock

Small holes at desired radii

Fig. 5   RADIUS TOOL

long as there are enough blocks so that two trains never get into the same one at the same time.

The boundaries between blocks must prevent electricity from passing along a rail into the next block. This is done by using plastic rail joiners instead of the usual metal ones at block boundary track joints. Block boundary locations are shown in fig. 6 as heavy black bars. The Bantam & Cycloid has five blocks.

Figs. 6 and 7 show the track feeders and power pack wiring for two-train operation on the B&C; the left pack runs one train while the right pack runs the other. There are five toggle switches of the double-pole, double-throw (dp.dt.) center-off type; each corresponds to one

of the five track blocks. Here's how a *block toggle* works:

The center position turns the block off. The left position connects the block to the left power pack for running train A. Note that any block or blocks can be assigned to the left pack to allow train A

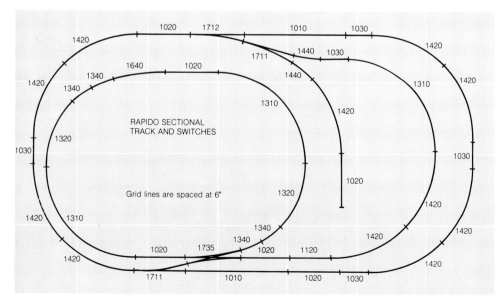

Fig. 4

B

A

1 x 2 lumber

1¼" x 12 flathead wood screws

FRAME DIMENSIONS	A	B
Layout No. 1	33"	18.5"
Layout No. 2	38"	22"
Layout No. 3	41.5"	22"

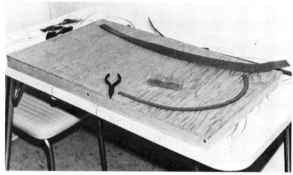

Fasten the cork strips with wire nails or staples. Start on one of the end curves.

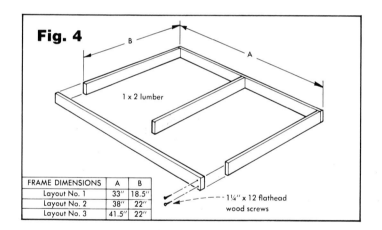

Fig. 3   TRACK REQUIRED (all Arnold Rapido)

(2) 1711, (1) 1712, (1) 1735, (2) 1010, (6) 1020, (5) 1030, (1) 1120, (11) 1420, (2) 1440, (3) 1310, (2) 1320, (4) 1340, (1) 1640, (7) Atlas or Midwest Products cork roadbed

Tracklaying is nearly complete in this photo. Note the wires from the switch machines. These will be led under the baseboard.

FRAMEWORK AND BASEBOARD

Quantity	Material	Use
2	1 x 2 No. 2 white pine, length A, fig. 4	Framework sides
3	1 x 2 No. 2 white pine, length B, fig. 4	Framework crossmembers
1	¼" interior plywood, dimensions A x B, fig. 4	Baseboard
1 doz.	1¼" No. 12 flathead wood screws	Framework fasteners
1 doz.	¾" No. 7 flathead wood screws	Baseboard to framework fasteners
White glue		

Tools

Saw (hand or power), screwdriver, hand or power drill with ⅛" twist drill bit, yardstick or folding rule, pencil

SCENERY MATERIALS

Quantity	Material	Use
	⅛" Masonite scraps	Tunnel lining, scenic profile boards, layout edging
2	Double-track tunnel portals	
1 roll	Masking tape	Protecting track
4 ft.	¹⁄₁₆" x ⅛" balsa strip	Form for road and station parking lot
	Paper towels	Hard-shell scenery
	Newspapers	Temporary support for hard-shell scenery
10 lbs.	Hydrocal or plaster of paris	Hard-shell scenery, zip texturing
	Dry pigment colors, 1 package each:	Zip texturing
	medium yellow	
	raw sienna	
	raw umber	
	burnt umber	
	dark green	
	Fabric dyes, 1 package each:	Zip texturing
	black	
	yellow	
	medium brown	
	dark brown	
	tan	
1 pkg.	N scale track ballast	
1 pt.	Acrylic matte medium	Ballast bonding
Liquid dishwashing detergent		

Tools

Mixing bowl, old spoon or spatula, coarse sieve

ROADBED, TRACK, AND WIRING SUPPLIES

Quantity	Material	Use
1 box	½" No. 20 wire brads	Track nails
1 doz.	Plastic rail joiners	Block insulation
1 box	⅜" wire staples	Roadbed fasteners
40 ft.	No. 22 electrical wire (20 feet each of two colors)	Block wiring
5	Double-pole, double-throw, center-off toggle switches	Block toggles
18 ft.	No. 22 electrical wire (six feet each of three colors)	Switch machine wiring
8	Miniature pushbuttons (4 each of two colors) single-pole, single-throw, normally open	Switch machine controls
1	⅛" Masonite panel, size to suit planned scenery (minimum about 8" x 10")	Control panel
2	Power packs, two required for two-train operation	

Track quantities shown with figures 1, 2, and 3

Tools

Small hammer, nail set, hobby knife, staple gun, soldering gun or iron, small roll 50-50 resin core solder, hand or power drill with bits to make holes for toggle switches and pushbuttons, small fine file, razor saw (for cutting flexible track sections, if used), needle-nose pliers, Kadee Quality Products No. 1055 N standards gauge (optional)

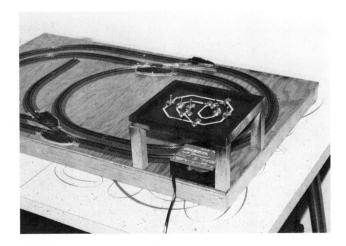

Extreme portability was a requirement for the B&C, so the control panel is built *into* the layout. The legless design reduces weight.

To prepare the layout for scenery, attach a thin profile board and place protective coverings on the track and control panel.

to run into them, or to run through them.

The right position of the toggle connects its block to the right power pack to run train B. The beauty of this block control scheme is that if your railroad expands, you don't add more power packs, only more toggle switches. The only time you need to add a third power pack is to run three trains. This method of wiring a layout is called "cab control wiring."

As you run a train from the left "cab," simply flip the toggles to the left for the blocks it enters; the second engineer, in the right cab, flips the toggles to the right as he needs the blocks. When your train clears a block, move the toggle to the center position so the other engineer will know that the block is available.

I built a small control panel into one corner of the mountain scenery to house the block toggles and the pushbuttons that control the electrically operated turnouts. This panel is made from 1/8"-thick Masonite.

Getting the gremlins out

This is a good point to stop and talk about some common model railroad problems. The quality of models and track components has improved to the point where you can expect the Bantam & Cycloid to run well right away, but here are some trouble spots to watch for after you've wired the railroad, or perhaps after you've operated for a few hours:

• **Locomotive won't run at all in one of the blocks.** There is an open circuit somewhere between the power pack and the track. Is the block toggle turned on? If so, trace the wires back from the track connections to the power pack. The most likely cause of an open circuit is a loose rail joiner or a poor wire connection at the track, block toggle, or power pack.

• **Locomotive runs until it reaches the insulated gaps between blocks, then stalls.** This indicates the two blocks are at opposite polarities. Check train operation in adjacent blocks to see which is wired for wrong direction. Interchange the block-toggle feeder wires (the center pair on the switch) for this block only.

• **Locomotive stalls at points within block boundaries around the layout.** This is most likely caused by poor rail joiner connections or dirty track. It is good practice to clean the track before each operating session. Several brands of track cleaners are offered at most hobby shops.

• **Derailments.** Derailments can be caused by improperly spaced wheels, poorly gauged track, or both. Some N scale equipment is notorious for improperly spaced wheels, so if one car derails at a spot where all other equipment passes freely, examine the wheels on that car. There are several ways to check wheel gauge. I suggest the Kadee standards gauge because it provides a means for checking trackwork as well. If you do find a poorly spaced wheelset,

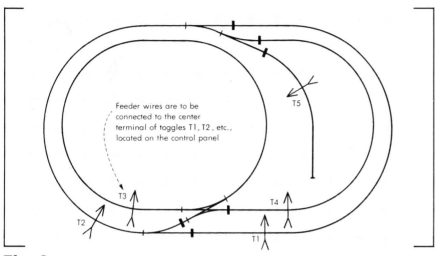

Fig. 6

Feeder wires are to be connected to the center terminal of toggles T1, T2, etc., located on the control panel

T5

T3

T4

T2

T1

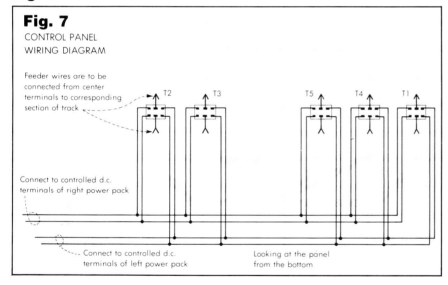

Fig. 7

CONTROL PANEL WIRING DIAGRAM

Feeder wires are to be connected from center terminals to corresponding section of track

T2   T3   T5   T4   T1

Connect to controlled d.c. terminals of right power pack

Connect to controlled d.c. terminals of left power pack

Looking at the panel from the bottom

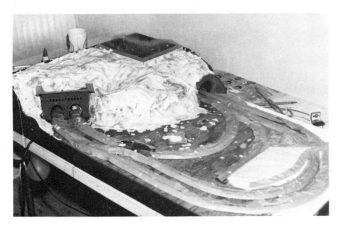

The basic hard shell is made by piling up wads of newspaper and covering them with plaster-soaked paper towels. It is self-supporting.

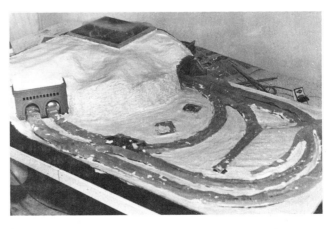

Another coat of plaster is used to smooth hard shell contours, blend in structure bases, and provide a base for rock carving.

most can be put in gauge by pulling or pushing one of the wheels while gently twisting it. If you encounter a difficult pair, replace it with a new set of wheels.

The more likely cause of derailments is the track. If more than one car derails at a track joint, run your fingers over the joint to feel for rough spots; these can be smoothed with a fine file. If the joint is on a curve, check to ensure that the rail ends are not sprung out of line. If they are, gently push them back into line with a screwdriver blade and spike them in place with a few scale spikes.

Gaps between rail ends, particularly on the outside of a curve, can derail anything that runs over them. The best solution is to remove the track pieces and realign them so there is no gap, but a *temporary* fix is possible: Just fill the gap with plastic wood or plastic model filler putty and trim to shape with a razor blade when dry. Finish the job with fine sandpaper.

Another type of derailment problem I've encountered is that certain brands of insulating plastic rail joiners are so thick that wheel flanges bump over them. A little razor blade trimming of the joiners solved this.

Derailments are common at turnouts, and the first place to look for trouble is at the points, the bladelike moving parts of the switch. See if there is any foreign matter preventing the points from fitting tightly against the stock (outside) rails, or jamming the throw rod. If the throw rod is binding for no apparent reason, try gently working the points back and forth with your fingers to free them. Occasionally you'll find points that are too thick or higher than the stock rails; even though they fit snugly against the stock rails, the wheels will pick at them. Use a fine file to feather these points slightly.

Hard-shell terrain

After the layout wiring is installed and checked, you'll probably spend some time running trains before finishing the layout. When you're ready for more work, the next step is scenery construction.

I began this phase of construction by cutting strips of Masonite to trim the edges of the layout frame. At the control panel end I shaped the strips to form a profile board for the mountainous scenery I had planned. The exact height and shape of this profile board is not critical.

Next, I installed the tunnel portals and a Masonite tunnel lining, then I covered the track with masking tape to prevent it from becoming coated with plaster.

The hard-shell method of building plaster scenery is quick, easy, and produces realistic results. You'll need some old newspapers, paper towels (the coarse type used in gas stations and public rest rooms are the best), plaster, a squeeze-pump sprayer, and an old

To make a road and parking area for the B&C, start by placing balsa forms as shown here.

Use a palette knife to smooth your "paved" surface. Keep it at or below rail level.

mixing bowl. Several types of plaster are suitable; I used a very strong kind called Hydrocal. This is sometimes difficult to find in small quantities, but some hobby shops stock it, or at least can tell you where to purchase some. Plaster of paris, also sold as molding plaster, is easier to find. The difference between plaster of paris and Hydrocal is that you'll need a thicker shell of plaster of paris to match the strength of a Hydrocal shell of a given thickness. Also, plaster of paris is less expensive in small quantities.

Arrange crumpled wads of newspaper to the shape of the hills or mountains on your layout, wetting with water from the sprayer bottle if the paper won't hold the shape you want. Mix two cups of dry plaster into one cup of water. If you have the right ratio of plaster to water the resulting mixture should have a consistency about like pancake batter.

Tear a strip of paper towel about 3″ x 8″ and swish it through your plaster mixture so that the "batter" sticks to both sides, then lay the strip over your newspaper wads. Add more strips, overlapping slightly, until the entire contour is covered. The plaster will harden in an hour, ready for texturing.

Zip texturing

To give color and life to the scenic contours, we'll use a process called "zip texturing." This consists of four techniques—all very easy to do—that almost automatically produce very lifelike scenic effects. The steps are, briefly:

1. Paint on a thin coat of plaster, making your brush strokes go in the same direction to represent horizontal or tilted rock strata, or stippling the surface with the tips of the bristles to represent granite.

2. Spray a dye solution onto the plaster to color the "rock."

3. Re-wet the plaster and sift dry plaster onto it everywhere. Use earth-colored dry plaster for soil and green-colored dry plaster for grassy patches.

4. Run water across the surface and down the hollows to create realistic erosion effects. Then repeat processes 1 through 4 until you are satisfied that you have results that look natural,

The completed road seems to "fit" on the layout because it was built in place.

rather than man-made. One of the strongest selling points for this scenic finishing technique is that tedious rock "carving" is unnecessary—a good thing, since the carving usually looks artificial.

Now for the details. The plaster coat is the same batterlike mix we used before, but this time molding plaster is preferred because it takes dye colors better than Hydrocal. Paint a coat of thin plaster over the hardened terrain, and, while it is setting, use the sprayer bottle to apply diluted fabric dyes. You can put pigment colors into the plaster batter, if you prefer, but the color should be kept very light and you should plan on applying dye coloring with a brush or sprayer as well. The trouble with putting the color into the plaster is that the result is too uniform, making your rocks look like castings made from plaster.

Buy black, yellow, and several brown and tan shades of dye. The type of dye you need is sold in dime, drug, and grocery stores under the trade names Rit, Tintex, and Putnam, and several others. Dilute the darker colors, but use yellows at almost full strength. Spray these over your terrain, one color at a time. Vary the colors and above all, strive for a mottled, non-uniform look. Use more brown for one kind of rock, more diluted black for another, but as a rule use at least three colors of dye for each part of your terrain. The color will settle and be darker in crevices and on rough textured surfaces, and will show up lighter where the plaster is smooth and hard. Most real rock is very light in tone—usually about as dark as concrete block—so be careful to not overdo the dye effects. If you do get overly dark areas, spray them with a little diluted bleach to lighten the bad effects.

Dry colors are the "zip" in zip texturing, and they come next. The dry colors are simply powdered pigments shaken in a jar with dry plaster until you get a realistic and pleasing shade of earth or grass. Plain pigments are best because they contain no glue, but you can use powdered water paints in a pinch. The problem with the powdered paints is that they might prevent the plaster from setting up hard unless you apply some kind of sealer to the terrain before the zip texturing.

You will need medium yellow, raw sienna, raw umber, burnt umber, and dark green pigment colors. If your hobby shop does not stock these dry powdered pigments, try an art-supply store. Mix the colors with dry plaster to obtain two or three earth browns and at least one green for grass. Usually yellow should be added to all mixtures to relieve the intense pigment colors. You will find that a relatively small amount of color is sufficient for most soil and grass colors. At least 25 per cent of the dry mixture should be plaster.

To apply the texturing, wet the hard-shell terrain and dust the soil color over it everywhere, using a spoon as an agitator to make the powder mixture fall through the mesh of a coarse sieve. The moisture will soak into the dry dust from beneath and cause it to harden in place. The earth mixture will cling to horizontal rock ledges and cover all reasonably level surfaces in a realistic manner. If, after an hour, the texture has not hardened to a surface that resists gentle brushing, mist more water onto it. This second water spray is often required in dry climates.

Now re-wet the terrain and dust on the grass-colored plaster-and-pigment mixes as you did the earth. Leave a few bare spots here and there, but sift the green mixture over most of the same places that you treated with the earth texture. If your layout represents a summertime western scene, use a dried grass color.

Hard-shell, zip texturing, and many other scenery techniques are explained and illustrated in detail in Kalmbach's SCENERY FOR MODEL RAILROADS, available at your hobby shop.

Roads, track ballast, and details

You can build the road leading to the passenger station and the station parking lot before or after the rest of the scenery is added. I built a form of $1/16''$ x $1/8''$ balsawood strips and poured plaster into it right on the layout. After the plaster had set, I sanded it smooth, cut flangeways into the grade crossing, and painted the surface light gray.

Track ballast can be added before or after your scenery is built, but I prefer to do it after. That way, the ballast overlaps the earth and grass textures just as it does on real railroads. Several brands of N scale ballast are available at most hobby shops, and there are several methods of fixing it to your roadbed. Here is how to ballast your track using the *bonded ballast method:*

1. Apply ballast dry, pouring it into the space between the rails from a creased paper cup or a spoon. Use the tip of your finger or a small brush to spread it around and between the ties, and brush it away from the railhead. Build up a ballast shoulder around the outside ends of the ties, but keep the ballast away from the working parts of the switches.

2. Mix a solution of water and liquid detergent (liquid dishwashing detergent works fine), one capful of detergent per gallon of water. Fill your sprayer bottle with this solution and spray several feet of the ballasted track with it. Mist on the spray only enough to dampen, not wet, the ballast.

3. Mix a solution of one part acrylic matte medium to six parts water. Thinned white glue can also be used for this bonding process, but the result is very hard and somewhat glossy. The acrylic matte medium makes the ballast compound much more resilient. You can find this acrylic material in all art and craft stores, many hobby shops, and some hardware stores. Use an eye-dropper to apply the solution to the damp ballast at intervals of every four or five ties. The milky liquid will spread throughout the ballast by capillary action aided by the wetting qualities of the detergent in the water spray. Continue wetting sections of ballasted track and applying the matte medium solution until the job is complete.

4. After the ballasting is complete, allow the solution to dry overnight and clean any traces of adhesive or ballast from the rails before running trains.

I finished my version of the Bantam & Cycloid by adding the four structures shown in the photos. There's room for several more along with a few trees, shrubs, vehicles, and figures. I accomplished my goal—my friend admitted after all that he did have room for a layout—and had a good time in the bargain.

If you enjoyed building this N scale railroad, you may want to try building a larger layout in the future. I built such a layout—the 4 x 6-foot Hoosier Southern—a few years ago, and its construction is described in detail in the book N SCALE PRIMER.

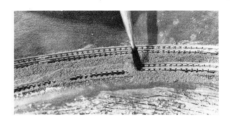

Above: Spread ballast with a brush. Below: After applying wetting solution to the ballast, add matte medium with an eye-dropper.

Keep ballast out of moving turnout parts.

There are many detail and accessory items available in N scale, and the completed B&C shows just how much interest they can generate in even a 2 x 4 layout.

Not just a layout, but a family hobby

The Christmas train set is only the beginning

Realistic point-to-point track design

Six industrial spurs plus an engine terminal

All turnouts operated remotely

Like challenges? You can add switching problems

From Train Set to Model Railroad

BY THE MODEL RAILROADER STAFF

ARE you looking for an activity you can enjoy at home throughout the year—something, perhaps, in which the whole family can participate? Maybe you're just looking for a hobby for yourself. Consider building the Marquette & Independence, a compact but action-packed model railroad we've designed with the beginner in mind.

We chose to build the M&I in HO scale, the most popular size with the greatest supply of products. Also, HO equipment is easier for a youngster to handle and work on because it is larger than N scale. Of course, do consider N scale too. In N scale you could build the M&I in a 2 x 7-foot space. N scale is the second most popular modeling size, and there is a good supply of equipment available. To build the layout in N scale you can follow the same general methods that we'll demonstrate for HO, but for additional information on con-struction aspects peculiar to N scale we recommend Kalmbach's N SCALE PRIMER by Russ Larson.

The track plan

The key premise of the Marquette & Independence is simplicity: We set out to find what it would take to develop a train set—such as might be purchased or received by a novice—into a realistic operating model railroad. We wanted to take the beginning modeler from the boredom he eventually finds with round-the-Christmas-tree running and start him on the road to scale model railroading. The M&I's design is simple, but its features have been thought out to allow the builder and operator to experience the many aspects of model railroading and develop talents in benchwork, tracklaying, wiring, and scenery construction.

We began with a train set which con-tained a loop of track with one turnout. Our set was from Cox, but most HO sets furnish about the same components. We added more turnouts and sectional and flexible track sections. We chose the dogbone loop design because it provides for continuous operation; point-to-point layouts generally don't suit the starting modeler unless the run between termi-nals is quite long.

The M&I represents a shortline or branchline railroad, and on our version we restricted operations to freight trains. The layout will accommodate 15 to 20 freight cars and two locomotives. Engine servicing facilities are the bare minimum required. The track plan fea-tures six industrial spurs—seven if you count the engine servicing track next to the drill track—and some spurs are long enough to handle more than one industry. Another important feature is the interchange at Prairie Junction, where the M&I trades cars with a con-necting railroad. Any type of car can be delivered to or picked up from this track, making it the most versatile sid-ing on the layout. The overall plan for the railroad is very flexible in that the loop can be split at the neck to expand the layout into a "U," "E," or "Z" shape, with any desired length of track along the legs; see fig 2.

Benchwork

The support for the Marquette & In-dependence follows what we call L-gir-der construction, with one major excep-tion: We added a flat tabletop for ease in construction and structure placement. Make the L-girders first, two at a time. Clamp two 1 x 4 boards together, spread white glue along the edge of *one* of them, and lay a 1 x 2 flat side down as shown in the photos. Drive 1¼" No. 8 screws through the 1 x 2 into the glued 1 x 4 to pull the boards together, and turn the assembly over. Apply glue to the other 1 x 4 and add another 1 x 2 to make the second girder.

We used a special countersinking bit in a ¼" power drill to speed this assem-bly. These bits are available in hard-ware stores in sizes to match standard wood screws. With these bits you can drill a small pilot hole for the screw threads, a larger clearance hole for the shank, and a tapered countersink that matches the underside of the head, all in one operation. Screws are easier to drive if the proper-size hole has been made, and they will maintain maximum hold-ing power. Scrape the threads across a bar of ordinary hand soap to lubricate screws for easier driving. We used both a Yankee spiral screwdriver and a screwdriver bit attachment mounted in a ¼" drill power clutch to save time and effort.

Make the layout tabletop of ½" plywood, cut according to fig. 4. Cut a 24" x 48" piece of ½" plywood (from your lumberyard's "short" bin) in half the

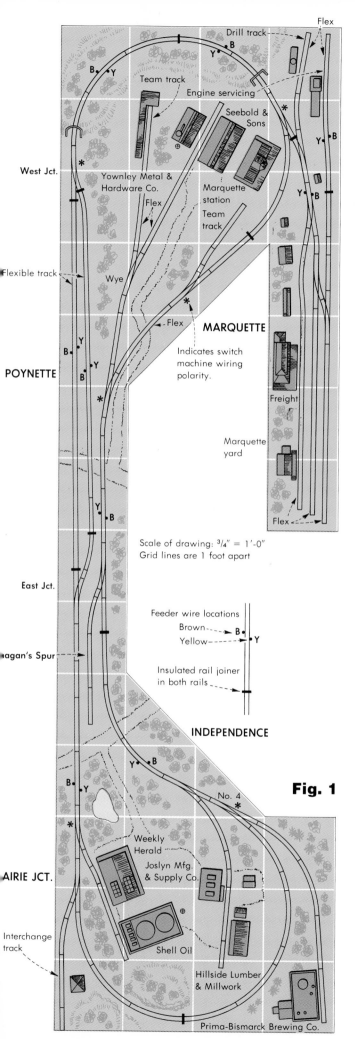

Fig. 1

Drill track

Flex

B

Y

Team track

Engine servicing

Seebold & Sons

*

West Jct.

Yownley Metal & Hardware Co.

Flex

Marquette station
Team track

Y · B

Flexible track

Wye

Flex

MARQUETTE

Indicates switch machine wiring polarity.

POYNETTE

B · Y

B · Y

*

Freight

Marquette yard

Scale of drawing: ³/₄" = 1'-0"
Grid lines are 1 foot apart

Flex

East Jct.

Feeder wire locations

Brown---- B ·

Yellow----· Y

·agan's Spur

Insulated rail joiner in both rails----

INDEPENDENCE

Y · B

B · Y

No. 4
*

AIRIE JCT.

Weekly Herald

Joslyn Mfg. & Supply Co.

Interchange track

Shell Oil

Hillside Lumber & Millwork

Prima-Bismarck Brewing Co.

Any train set can serve as a starting point for a model railroad empire like our Marquette & Independence. We used this Cox train set for our project layout, but it is only one of many brands that are suitable for the job.

Here's a preview of the finished layout — a long freight rumbles down the main while a switcher (out of the photo) works Marquette yard. Independent two-train operation and plenty of industrial switching make running the M&I interesting — and fun!

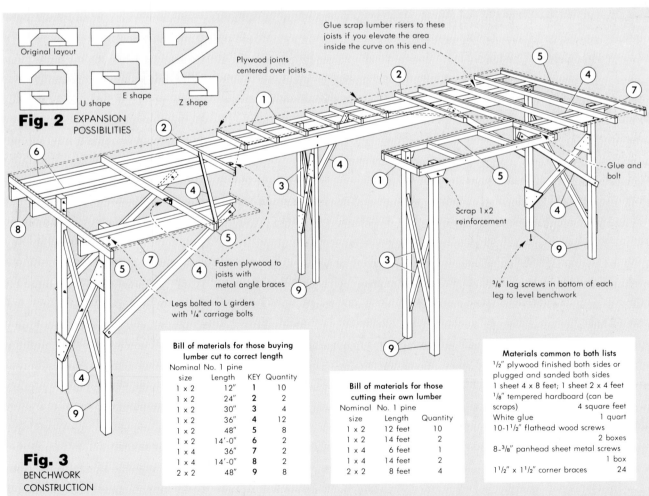

Original layout

U shape   E shape   Z shape

Fig. 2 EXPANSION POSSIBILITIES

Glue scrap lumber risers to these joists if you elevate the area inside the curve on this end

Plywood joints centered over joists

Glue and bolt

Scrap 1x2 reinforcement

³/₈" lag screws in bottom of each leg to level benchwork

Fasten plywood to joists with metal angle braces

Legs bolted to L girders with ¹/₄" carriage bolts

Fig. 3
BENCHWORK
CONSTRUCTION

Bill of materials for those buying lumber cut to correct length
Nominal No. 1 pine

size	Length	KEY	Quantity
1 x 2	12"	1	10
1 x 2	24"	2	2
1 x 2	30"	3	4
1 x 2	36"	4	12
1 x 2	48"	5	8
1 x 2	14'-0"	6	2
1 x 4	36"	7	2
1 x 4	14'-0"	8	2
2 x 2	48"	9	8

Bill of materials for those cutting their own lumber
Nominal No. 1 pine

size	Length	Quantity
1 x 2	12 feet	10
1 x 2	14 feet	2
1 x 4	6 feet	1
1 x 4	14 feet	2
2 x 2	8 feet	4

Materials common to both lists
¹/₂" plywood finished both sides or plugged and sanded both sides
1 sheet 4 x 8 feet; 1 sheet 2 x 4 feet
¹/₈" tempered hardboard (can be scraps)   4 square feet
White glue   1 quart
10-1¹/₂" flathead wood screws
                                      2 boxes
8-³/₈" panhead sheet metal screws
                                      1 box
1¹/₂" x 1¹/₂" corner braces   24

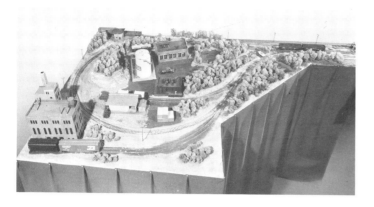

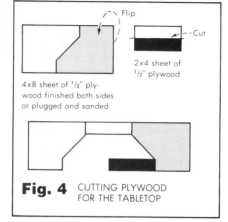

Fig. 4 CUTTING PLYWOOD FOR THE TABLETOP

Your first step in benchwork construction will be to fashion L-girders. These light and rigid support members are made by fastening a 1 x 2 to the edge of a 1 x 4 with white glue and screws. Study the photos and note how two girders are built at the same time; this makes the lumber easier to handle. To save time, we drilled the holes for the screws with a countersinking pilot bit and a ¼" power drill, and drove the screws with a Yankee push-type spiral screwdriver. An even easier way to drive the screws is to use a clutch attachment with a screwdriver blade in the ¼" power drill.

long way to make two 12" x 48" pieces. One of these fits between the large end pieces and the other becomes the base for the freight yard. We did all the plywood cutting with a fine-tooth blade in a power saber saw, but the cuts are simple enough that you can use a crosscut hand saw. Wrap a sheet of medium sandpaper around a scrap 1 x 4 and use it to round off the sawed plywood edges. *Don't* try to do this with the sandpaper held over your fingers; the slivers will penetrate both the sandpaper and your skin!

Now lay the entire tabletop on the floor, making sure that all parts are positioned properly. Write the word "top" on each end piece so there will be no mistakes when you assemble the supports underneath.

Turn one tabletop section upside down and cut and mount the joists across it; see fig. 3. Fasten the top to the joists using 1½" x 1½" metal corner braces held in place with ⅜" No. 8 panhead sheet metal screws. Repeat the process for the other large tabletop section.

Install the joists across the center piece of plywood next, but be sure to leave space at the ends of the plywood section for the cleats that will join the plywood parts. Lay everything on the floor again, joist side up. Attach the 14-foot L-girders with 1¼" screws through the 1 x 2 flange at each of the joists.

Make the leg assemblies, using 2 x 2 legs and 1 x 2 cross bracing. We used scraps of ⅛" Masonite for the gusset plates, but ¼" plywood will also work. Use ⅜" No. 8 panhead sheet metal screws to attach the gussets, then bolt the leg assemblies to the L-girders with ¼" x 3" carriage bolts, nuts, and washers. Add the angle bracing from the legs to the L-girders as shown in fig. 3. We added leveling devices by drilling a ¹³⁄₆₄" hole and driving a ⅜" lag screw into the bottom of each leg, stopping with the head extending about ½".

Now lift the table and turn it right side up on its legs. Pause for a moment and admire your craftsmanship—benchwork construction is probably the biggest hurdle for most beginning model railroaders to overcome. With the really heavy work behind you, you're

All's quiet in the usually bustling Marquette yard while borrowed Santa Fe Geep No. 2232 idles on the ready track. The small sandhouse and the simple oil storage tank in the background are the sum total of locomotive facilities needed to service the M&I's roster of modern shortline motive power. Note how the sandhouse, oil tank, and Marquette station share a "family" gray-and-green color scheme.

now ready to lay the track and get the trains rolling.

Preparing to lay the track

First, draw grid lines on the plywood top at 1-foot intervals to correspond with the lines on the track plan, fig. 1. Using these lines as a guide, sketch the track plan in pencil on the tabletop. A yardstick with a hole drilled at the 18" mark is a handy device for marking in curved trackage. Assemble all the sectional track and see how it fits your penciled track plan. The parts do not have to fit your drawing exactly, but make sure that all of the track joints will line up properly without kinks. Temporarily tack the assembled track in position at several locations and draw center lines through the ties onto the plywood with a black felt-tip marker. Also use the marker to draw center lines for the flexible track sections.

Remove the track from the tabletop and install the cork roadbed over the track center lines. The material we used comes in 36" lengths with beveled edges, and is the correct width for single track. The roadbed is very flexible and can easily be shaped to conform to the track plan. Where necessary for a fit, cut the roadbed with a modeler's knife and tack it in place with ½" No. 19 wire nails.

After we had the roadbed down, but before we laid any track, we decided to slightly elevate the team track and the spurs leading to Yownley Metal & Hardware and Seebold & Sons. This step is optional, but it does make the layout more realistic. Here's how to do it: Mark a cut line on the plywood, allowing enough room alongside the tracks for the structures. Mark the position of the joists underneath the plywood surface so you don't saw through them when you make the cut. Drill a hole on the cut line between each pair of joists, large enough to accept a saber saw or keyhole saw blade. Insert the saw and cut through the plywood up to the joists, watching for any interfering metal angles (detach and move them away from the saw cut if they interfere). Carefully saw through the plywood at the joist positions by tilting the saw —don't cut the joists. If necessary, make final cuts with a keyhole saw to free the ballon-shaped section; however, remember that the neck of this "balloon" must remain attached to the rest of the table top. Glue ¾"- and ⁹⁄₁₆"-thick riser strips to the top of the joists as shown in fig. 3, and secure the raised portion with 1½" metal corner braces.

Track installation

Once you have the roadbed down,

The biggest sawing job in construction of the M&I is cutting the ½" plywood tabletop panels. You can do the job with a hand saw, but a fine-tooth saber saw is faster.

Here's our first section of benchwork. We assembled the parts upside down to make the work easier. If you follow the same procedure, remember that you'll need at least a two-man crew to turn the completed unit upright.

Tack the roadbed material over the track centerlines on the plywood tabletop with ½" No. 19 wire nails.

To raise this portion of the layout make saw cuts through the plywood as shown and add wood shims on top of the joists.

TRACKWORK BILL OF MATERIALS

(Total amount needed. Subtract the number of pieces in your train set)

Atlas track supplies

	Snap-Switches, remote-control
7	left hand
6	right hand
1	No. 4 turnout, left hand
1	wye turnout
2	remote-control switch machines for No. 4 and wye turnouts
	curved Snap-Track, 18" radius
19	full sections
3	half sections
8	third sections (one supplied with each Snap-Switch)
	straight Snap-Track
14	9" sections
8	6" sections
3	3" sections
3	1½" sections
7	curvable 36" sections
1 pkg.	insulated rail joiners

Materials from other suppliers

36 pcs.	cork roadbed, 36" lengths (we used roadbed for structure bases also)
1 box	wire nails, ½" No. 19
2 rolls ea.	Labelle wire, No. 24 AWG, 33-foot rolls
	No. 6002, yellow/brown, for block feeders
	No. 6003, green/yellow/red, for switch machines
1 pt.	acrylic polymer medium, matte finish
5	ballast, gray (main line), small bags (approx. 12 oz. by volume)
3	ballast, black (spurs and yard), small bags

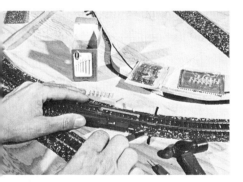

Begin tracklaying by installing the turnouts that lead into Marquette yard. Starting here will minimize misalignments in this critical area. Extra care and thoughtful, deliberate workmanship in tracklaying will pay off in reliable operation over the life of the layout.

you're ready to fasten the track permanently. Begin tracklaying with the turnouts leading into the yard. This is the most complicated trackwork on the layout, so it's best to put it down first and make the rest of the track align with it. Sectional track comes with mounting holes at each end and the middle, but on certain brands of turnouts you'll have to drill holes in the center of the ties for nails; see fig. 5. Use a hammer and a nail set to seat the ½" No. 19 wire nails. The underside of the nailheads should barely touch the tops of the ties as shown in fig. 6. If you pound them in too far you will distort the ties and narrow the track gauge, making derailments likely.

Poorly installed track means derail-

ments and frustration during the life of a model railroad, so work slowly and carefully. Make sure all rail joints are in line, and sight down the track frequently to detect —and eliminate— kinks. There are several locations where you must install insulated rail joiners as you lay the track. See fig. 1.

You'll have to cut the flexible track sections to length, and when the flex track is curved, one rail comes out longer and must be trimmed. Rail trimming can be done with a razor saw, a hand-held motor tool equipped with a cutting disk (be sure to wear safety glasses with this tool), or a good pair of flush-cutting nippers. The nippers are the easiest way to do the job. After you've trimmed the rails, undercut the tie strip under the rail ends with a razor saw so you can slip on rail joiners.

When two pieces of sectional track do not align perfectly, try cutting through a few of the short bars of plastic that join the ties. Doing this will make a portion of the track into a flexible section which

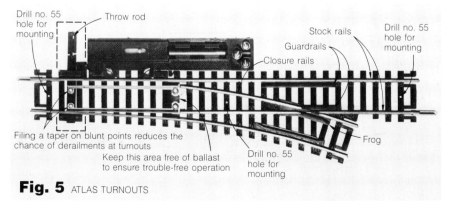

Drill no. 55 hole for mounting

Throw rod

Stock rails

Drill no. 55 hole for mounting

Guardrails

Closure rails

Filing a taper on blunt points reduces the chance of derailments at turnouts

Keep this area free of ballast to ensure trouble-free operation

Drill no. 55 hole for mounting

Frog

Fig. 5 ATLAS TURNOUTS

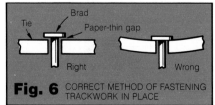

Tie — Brad — Paper-thin gap

Right — Wrong

Fig. 6 CORRECT METHOD OF FASTENING TRACKWORK IN PLACE

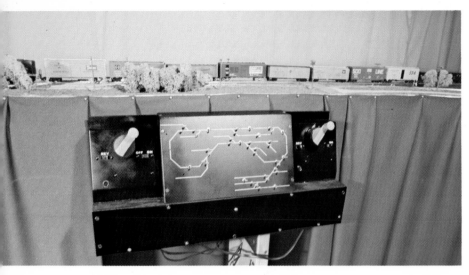

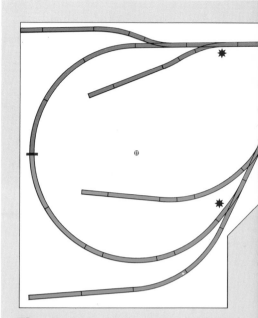

If you wire your version of the M&I for dual cab control, you'll need a control panel like this to organize power distribution and switch machine controls. Ours is near the center of the layout, where both engineers have a good view of the entire railroad. In our control scheme, the green pushbuttons in the layout schematic align the turnouts for the main line, while the red buttons route the trains into sidings, spurs, or yard trackage.

Fig. 7 PANEL TO LAYOUT WIRING

RAIL JOINTS AND SWITCH POINTS

Proper alignment of rail joints is critical to smooth and dependable operation. Make sure you have a tight fit in the rail joiners and that there are no obstructions at the joint to interfere with a wheel rolling across it. Use a jeweler's file to smooth the top and inside edge of each joint. Also, the gap between rail ends should be no greater than the thickness of one sheet of paper.

Carefully taper the inside ends of the switch points with a file. Sharpen and dress these areas to prevent wheels from "picking the points" and derailing.

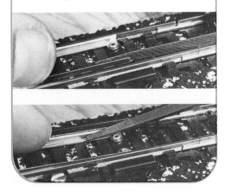

can be bent as required to suit the situation. This trick is especially handy where curved track sections do not form a smooth curve.

When you have all of the track in place, examine each rail joint. Slowly draw a fingertip across each joint and smooth any mismatch on the inside or top of the rails using a small file. Also file tapers on the blunt ends of all switch points to reduce the chances of derailments there.

Feeder and switch machine wiring

Install track feeder wires before ballasting the track so the ballast material will help disguise the connections. These feeders will be connected into our wiring scheme later, but for now all you have to know is what type of wire to use and where and how to install it.

You can use any type of stranded insulated wire that is No. 24 AWG or larger, up to about No. 16 AWG (a lower AWG number is *larger* wire). We used Labelle Industries hookup wire No. 6002, which has two conductors, one brown and one yellow, joined into a strip. Installation locations for track feeders are shown on the track plan, fig. 1, and on the panel-to-layout wiring diagram, fig. 7. You'll have to choose between cutting the wire into 3-foot lengths and splicing later, or cutting each feeder set to the length needed to reach the location you select for a centrally located control panel. The photo sequence shows how to install individual feeder wires at trackside.

Three wires must be connected to each switch machine, so we used Labelle three-wire strip No. 6003. The wires are color coded green, yellow, and red, and are connected as shown in fig. 8. Drill a $^5/_{32}''$ hole alongside each switch

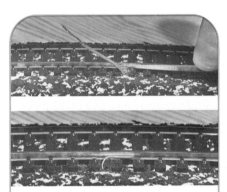

INSTALLING FEEDER WIRES

We installed feeder wires for each block before we ballasted the track. Drill a $^1/_{16}''$ hole outside the rail at the connection points shown on the track plan and run the wire up from underneath the layout. Strip about $^1/_2''$ of insulation from the end. Scrape the rail with a file to clean the area where the connecton will be made and bend the stripped end of the wire so it will lay alongside the rail. Use a hot soldering iron to apply solder to the wire and the rail, but don't linger with the iron or the plastic will melt. After the joint has cooled, use a file to remove any excess solder from the top of the railhead.

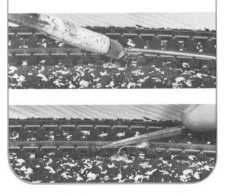

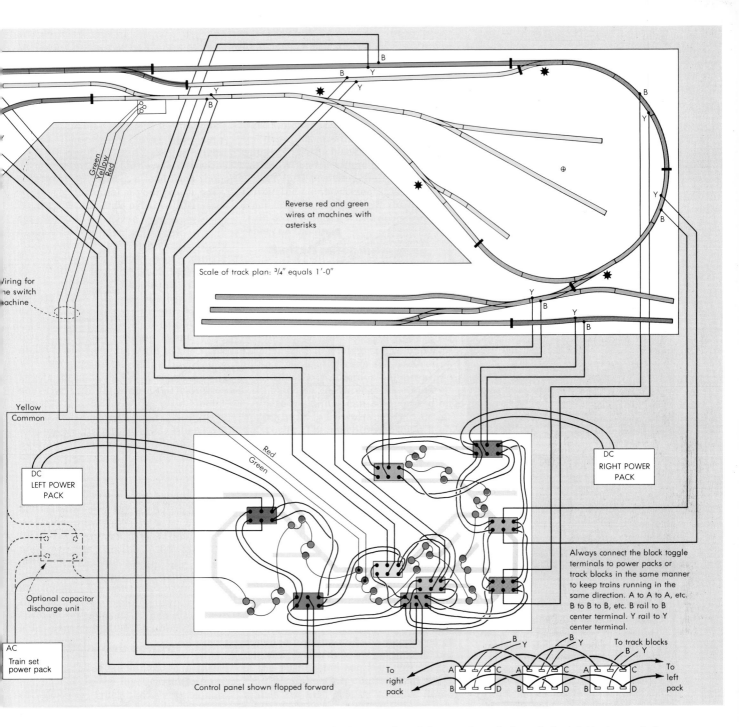

Green
Yellow
Red

B
Y
B
Y
B
Y
B
Y
B
Y

Reverse red and green
wires at machines with
asterisks

Scale of track plan: ³/₄" equals 1'-0"

Wiring for
the switch
machine

Yellow
Common

Red
Green

DC
LEFT POWER
PACK

DC
RIGHT POWER
PACK

Optional capacitor
discharge unit

Always connect the block toggle
terminals to power packs or
track blocks in the same manner
to keep trains running in the
same direction. A to A to A, etc.
B to B to B, etc. B rail to B
center terminal. Y rail to Y
center terminal.

AC
Train set
power pack

Control panel shown flopped forward

To
right
pack

B Y   B Y   To track blocks
              B Y

A ⌐ ⌐ ⌐ C   A ⌐ ⌐ ⌐ C   A ⌐ ⌐ ⌐ C
B ⌐ ⌐ ⌐ D   B ⌐ ⌐ ⌐ D   B ⌐ ⌐ ⌐ D

To
left
pack

machine and route the wires up from beneath the layout.

Ballasting the track

HO ballast is either fine sand or crushed rock colored and graded for uniformity. Several brands are available at hobby shops. We chose to ballast the track before adding scenery to the layout. We used the bonded ballast method described in the Bantam & Cycloid chapter, so refer to the B&C story for a detailed explanation of ballasting.

Cookbook wiring: getting one train running

Many newcomers to this hobby encounter a major pitfall when they come to the wiring phase of their first layout. Usually, they "have an idea" of how

their pike should be wired and forge ahead based on this "idea" rather than following instructions or a manual on the subject. We suggest the opposite approach—follow the directions and diagrams step-by-step and you'll have the trains running in a very short time. No

knowledge of electricity is needed, so let's proceed.

First, double-check to make sure you inserted plastic rail joiners at the locations designated in fig. 1. If you missed some (we did), it's not necessary to rip up any of your carefully ballasted track;

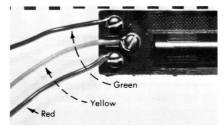

Green
Yellow
Red

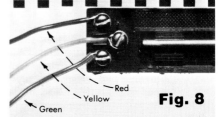

Red
Yellow
Green

Fig. 8

Wire most turnouts per the left diagram. Starred ones in fig. 1 follow the right diagram.

Above: For the basic terrain on the M&I we covered everything but the track with a shell of plaster-soaked paper towels. For hills, we wadded up newspaper as temporary support while the plaster set. For the tunnel between Marquette and West Junction, we built a rough support from Upson board with an opening at the rear for access, then plastered up to and over the "box."

To add rock strata on the flanks of the tunnel, apply a thick, claylike plaster coat and carve it with a putty knife. Work the plaster with the blade of the knife until it looks rugged and convincing, then brush on a very thin coat of watery plaster to round the contours slightly.

rug or welcome mat near the layout so you can wipe your feet before you leave the area and prevent plaster from being tracked all over the house.

We used plaster of paris rather than the somewhat stronger Hydrocal because it was easier to obtain. Mix small batches of plaster until you gain an appreciation of how fast it sets and how rapidly you can work with it. Start by pouring 1 cup of water into your mixing bowl and add plaster until the mixture is about the consistency of soupy pancake batter, normally about 2 parts plaster to 1 part water. Use a rubber spatula to mix the "soup."

We covered the entire layout with plaster—even the flat areas—to create a uniform surface texture and a good base for coloring. We wadded up plaster-soaked toweling here and there to add a little relief to the open sections of the scene. Work the plaster right up to the edge of the tape that protects the track, but keep in mind that any plaster that overlaps the edge of the tape will crack off when the tape is removed later, and you will have to touch up the area.

Because traces of hardened plaster speed up the setting time of newly mixed plaster, clean your mixing bowl after several batches have been mixed. Keep a large basin or bucket of water handy for cleaning the mixing bowl and your hands, and deposit hardened chunks of plaster in the garbage to avoid clogging any plumbing.

Tunnel construction

Before you can start plastering over the tunnel area, some type of enclosure

should be built over the track. Ours shown in the photos was made of ⅛" Masonite tacked to scrap 1 x 2 supports. The design and dimensions are not critical. Just be sure to allow adequate clearance for trains inside, and leave an access opening at the rear so you can reach the trains in case of a derailment.

We bought a commercial portal for one end of the tunnel, and simulated a natural rock entrance at the other end by troweling plaster around a bottle stuck in the opening to create an arch. Before the plaster fully set, we removed the bottle and carved around the newly formed entrance with an X-acto knife (a thin screwdriver blade or putty knife would also work) to simulate rugged rock. Afterwards we wet the hard-shell covering around the carved tunnel portal, applied about ¼" of thickened plaster over it, and carved it to match the portal. After we created a convincing rocklike surface on the tunnel opening and the adjoining areas, we brushed watery plaster over it to smooth the surface slightly.

Texturing techniques

We used two methods of coloring and texturing the hardened plaster shell on the M&I: zip texturing, which is explained in the Bantam & Cycloid chapter along with hard-shell scenicking, and fiber texturing, in which ground earth and grass materials are used.

Before you add either type of texturing, spray the plaster with watered down dyes so that no glaring white plaster will show in areas that are not 100

The natural-looking rock portal at the West Junction end of the M&I's tunnel was made by plastering around a bottle and a few wood scraps, then carving strata. Note how the rockwork extends into the tunnel mouth just enough to make the tunnel look solid.

per cent textured. We used yellow, red, and black Rit dyes, and other brands of powdered fabric dyes will work just as well. Add a pinch of black dye to a hand sprayer bottle full of water, and color all the plaster gray. Next spray some of the rocks and steeply sloping areas with red and yellow dye solutions. These sloping areas will become exposed rock and earth once the texturing is completed.

If you plan to use zip texturing, refer to the Bantam & Cycloid chapter for a list of the steps involved. Also, Bill McClanahan's SCENERY FOR MODEL RAILROADS, published by Kalmbach, gives detailed coverage of the zip-texturing process.

Fiber texturing is quite different from zip, and the adhesive and color/texture are applied in separate steps. We used a brownish-green ground cover consisting of 3 parts Life-Like earth to 1 part Life-Like grass, but colored sawdust or colored shredded foam material also could be used.

Follow these steps for fiber texturing:

1. Spread diluted white glue (1 part white glue to 1 part water) over several square feet of the layout with an old paint brush.

2. Sprinkle the ground-cover mixture over the white glue and pat it gently to ensure that the texture material contacts the glue. Use plenty of the texture; the excess will be recovered and used again. Continue applying ground cover until your work session is over and let dry overnight.

3. Put a clean bag in a vacuum cleaner and vacuum up any loose ground cover.

4. If the coverage is spotty, repeat steps 1 through 3 in those areas.

After you have textured the entire layout, remove the tape from the track

area. Vacuum up excess plaster particles and texture materials, and touch up any ragged edges with a small amount of plaster and texture over them.

Roads—and a pond

We simulated asphalt roads on the M&I by applying black furnace cement over the textured hard shell. This technique worked well except in some areas where we spread the cement too thin. Here, the cement cracked and broke up, resembling a frost-heaved country road after a hard winter. Rather than repair our cracked road, we used it as an excuse to put an HO road crew to work.

We used brown N scale ballast for gravel roads, bonding it in place with the ballasting procedure.

We included a pond near the *Weekly Herald* building. We formed banks about ½" thick from solid plaster and, after texturing, painted the bottom a dark blue-green. Then we poured the "form" full of clear plastic casting resin, the kind used for craft projects. The brands we've used all gave off a terrible odor while setting, so plan to pour your pond at a time when the family can leave the house for a few hours, and open the windows before mixing the resin.

Trees, foliage, and details

Although many types of attractive ready-built trees are available at most hobby shops, foresting even a small layout with them becomes quite expensive. We fashioned several dozen very simple trees from brown coated nails and lichen. We used some of the coarse lichen pieces to simulate small bushes and low growth by gluing them directly to the scenery.

Two different texturing techniques make for extra variety in your scenery. Above, far left, we're using a fine strainer to apply plaster and pigment "zip texture" in the area around Independence. The other three photos show how to apply sawdust and ground foam rubber texture materials using thinned white glue. Both methods are effective.

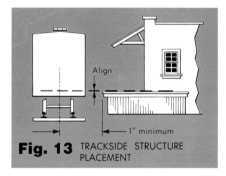

Fig. 13 TRACKSIDE STRUCTURE PLACEMENT

Hundreds of details can be added to your layout; people, vehicles, animals, litter, signs, phone poles—anything found in the real world around a railroad. A very wide range of figures and details are available in HO scale, and adding or rearranging a few of them from time to time is part of the continuing fun of our model railroad hobby.

The realistically cracked and potholed paved roads on the M&I were a mistake! We made them by applying a thin coat of furnace cement — just a bit *too* thin as it turned out.

Paint the pond bottom and let it dry thoroughly before you add the plastic resin "water."

Space-Saving Layout Storage Ideas

Three approaches to making your layout disappear: Foldaway, hideaway, flip-top

Don't let lack of space prevent you from building a layout; others have built model railroads in attaché cases and desk drawers! The ideas on these pages offer unorthodox solutions to the problem of "no place for the railroad"—a problem that has confronted *every* model railroader at one time or another.

The drawings and photographs here are not intended as detailed, step-by-step instructions and plans to build a foldaway, flip-top, or hideaway model railroad. We've chosen this material to give you designs that you can tailor to the space you have and the layout you want to build. Exact dimensions, materials, and construction are up to you. Some modelers have finished the non-railroad side of a space-saving layout like these to match the paneling or furniture in the room, so the possibilities are far from limited, even for apartment and mobile-home dwellers.

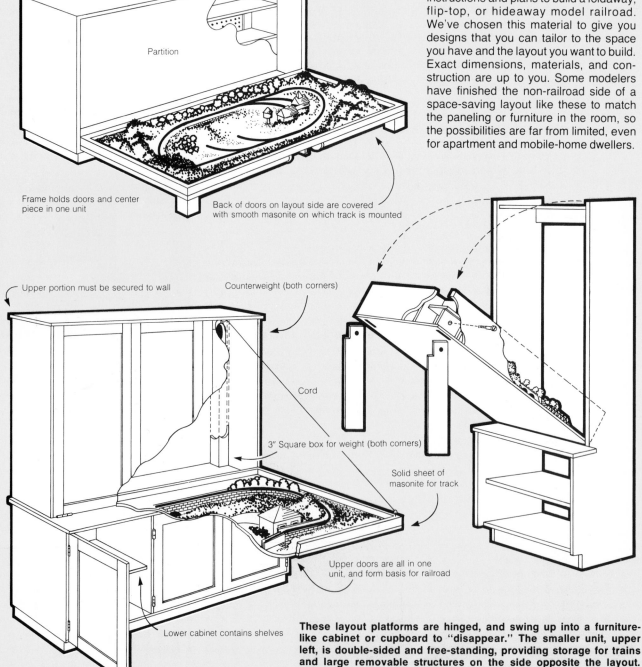

Partition

Frame holds doors and center piece in one unit

Back of doors on layout side are covered with smooth masonite on which track is mounted

Upper portion must be secured to wall

Counterweight (both corners)

Cord

3" Square box for weight (both corners)

Solid sheet of masonite for track

Upper doors are all in one unit, and form basis for railroad

Lower cabinet contains shelves

Lower doors are hinged at the sides

These layout platforms are hinged, and swing up into a furniture-like cabinet or cupboard to "disappear." The smaller unit, upper left, is double-sided and free-standing, providing storage for trains and large removable structures on the side opposite the layout. The larger cabinets are designed to be fastened to the wall, and the layout at left uses window sash counterweights to make raising and lowering the layout easier.

The butt-jointed framework for this flip-top design is pivoted at each end and supported on a double A-frame stand. These A-frames support the weight of the layout in both positions; two small drop legs stabilize the pike when it is horizontal. Casters allow the layout to be rolled close to a wall when flipped vertical. The simple roll-away design is adequate for layouts up to 5 x 9 feet, but larger pikes should be permanently mounted like the hideaway layout, below. For stability, the bases of the A-frame stands should be at least half their height, and the casters must be of sufficient size to carry the weight of the completed scenicked layout. At least one layout has been built to a design similar to this with a different pike on each side of the framework—now *that's* using space efficiently!

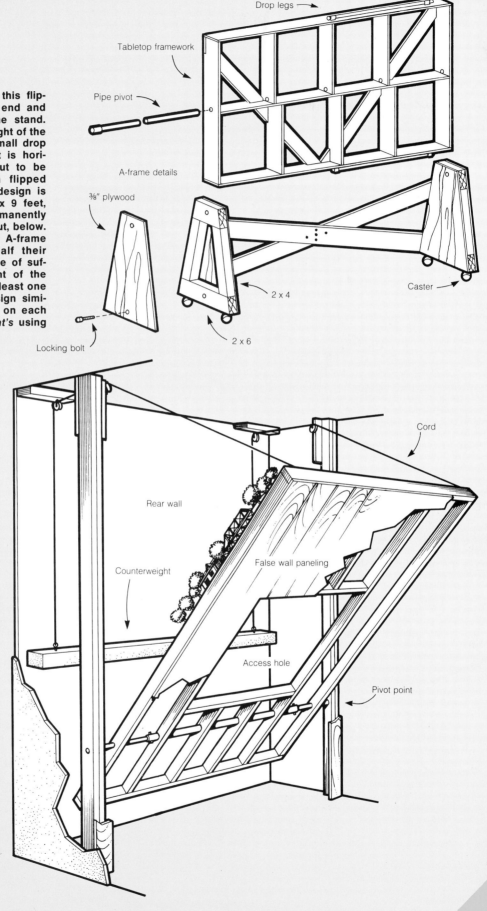

Drop legs

Tabletop framework

Pipe pivot

A-frame details

⅜" plywood

Locking bolt

2 x 6

2 x 4

Caster

This disappearing layout design folds up into the wall much like the old hideaway Murphy beds. It is the largest of the three types, so large that it requires a free-standing framework. The pop-up opening in the center of the layout can be covered with a mirror or picture. This design has been successfully used for for an 8 x 10-foot HO layout which takes up only 26" along one wall of a room.

Placement of the pivot point in this design is an important consideration, its height will determine the working height of the layout and the amount of room the unit will require when stored. Special attention must also be given to rigidity of the framework and overall layout weight, especially if you plan to employ plaster scenic techniques.

Advantages common to all these disappearing layouts are: they won't be exposed to hot, cold, humid, and dry environments common in cellars, attics, and garages; they protect the layout from pets, toddlers, and careless visitors when in the storage position; and the requirement to tilt them for storage helps prevent the layout from becoming a catch-all between operating sessions.

Cord

Rear wall

Counterweight

False wall paneling

Access hole

Pivot point

A layout for apartment dwellers—in **N** or **HO**

It's built—and stored—in a clothes closet

Two mines, a town, and a junction in 2x4

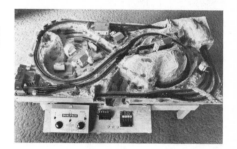

The Rubble Creek & Thunder Mine Railroad

BY MICHAEL GRUTSCH

FACED with the confines of apartment living, my ambition of building a model railroad never got past the dream stage until I discovered N scale. When I held an N scale train set in my hands, I knew there should be some way to build a small layout, efficiency apartment or not!

After giving the matter of location considerable thought, I chose a clothes closet. There were several advantages in this choice. First, because the closet

doors can be removed and replaced easily, I gained several important inches of layout length. By mounting the simple layout benchwork on casters I was able to roll the table out of the closet to work on it, and roll it away for storage. During construction, this keeps the layout and construction materials out of the way, and after the pike is completed the closet storage helps keep the layout free from house dust.

The 12-inch height of the 2 x 4-foot

table provides limited storage space beneath the layout, but does not interfere with garments hanging above. I hinged the control panel to the front of the frame to allow it to swing down out of the way when not in use. The track was laid over cork roadbed strip, and I made the scenery using plaster over window screen. Layout construction took only 84 hours, but the time was spread out over a year and a half.

The track plan includes 25 feet of track (not quite a scale mile) and ten turnouts. The passing siding, six spurs, and seven permanent uncoupling ramps provide enough switching to keep things interesting.

I consider the layout complete, but there's still some lettering to do and a few more small structures to build. The station and general store at Wecen are scratchbuilt, while the rest of the structures are plastic kits.

	N version	HO version
Size of squares	8″	16″
Layout length	4′-0″	8′-0″
Layout width	2′-0″	4′-0″
Minimum radius	8″	16″

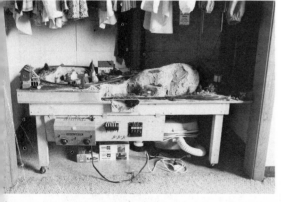

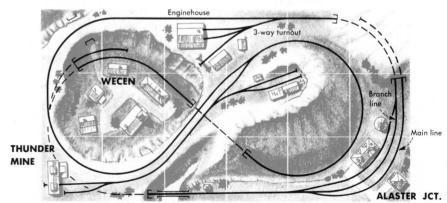